Succeed in
IELTS Life Skills

CEFR **B1**

Speaking & Listening

MP3 download

Andrew Betsis
Sean Haughton

GlobalELT

Published by GLOBAL ELT LTD
www.globalelt.co.uk
Copyright © **GLOBAL ELT LTD, 2015**

Andrew Betsis and Lawrence Mamas
Contributors: Maria Georgopoulou and Linda Maria Windsor

Every effort has been made to trace the copyright holders and we apologize in advance for any unintentional omission.
We will be happy to insert the appropriate acknowledgements in any subsequent editions.

● Succeed in IELTS Life Skills - CEFR Level B1 - Speaking & Listening - Student's Book - ISBN: 978-1-78164-272-6

CONTENTS

IELTS Life Skills - Level B1

About the IELTS Life Skills test for the B1 level

Phase 1a	Have a short discussion for about 2 minutes on a familiar topic with your partner.	3 min
Phase 1b	First, make some notes and then talk **on your own** about a familiar topic for one and a half minutes. Then, answer three questions your partner asks you about your talk. Listen to your partner talk for about one and a half minutes. Ask your partner three questions about their talk.	7 min
Phase 2a	Listen to 2 short recordings. First, listen for the general topic and choose an answer from 3 options. Then, listen again for 2 pieces of specific information.	5 min
Phase 2b	You are given a situation to talk about with your partner for two minutes. You must discuss the situation and agree on what to do. The examiner will give you a prompt card with things that you should discuss. **(3 min)** You are then given a related topic to talk about with your partner. This is a general discussion where you share ideas and opinions. **(4 min)**	7 min
Total Time		22 min

- This exam tests your Speaking and Listening skills. You do not have to write anything down. For example, when you finish listening to the recording in the Listening section, you say your answers.

- You will take the exam with another student. You will have to work together – you will need to discuss topics, listen to one another and ask each other questions.

- In Phase 1, you will talk about familiar or personal topics. In Phase 2, you will listen to and talk about more general topics.

- The topics covered in this exam are:
  - Personal details and experiences
  - Education/training
  - Health
  - Leisure
  - Buying goods
  - Housing
  - Family and friends
  - Transport
  - Work
  - Weather

About this book

In this book, there are 8 theme-based preparation sections designed to introduce you to topic-relevant vocabulary, remind you of some important grammar points and get you practising your speaking skills as much as possible.

These are followed by 8 relevant exam preparation units. There is an exam preparation unit to go with each of the 8 sections. This unit should be completed when you have finished the related section. It always has Listening practice on the unit's topic and additional exam-style speaking activities.

At the end of this book, there are 6 practice tests. The tests are scripted for the examiner. The information the student can see on the day of the exam is highlighted. Keep this in mind while you practise.

Using as a Self-study Book

For an exam that involves quite a lot of pair work, it is important to practise discussion activities. Therefore, many of the speaking activities in this book are designed to be done with a partner. However, if you have not got a partner, you need to be imaginative in how you practise. That may even involve creating an 'imaginary partner': a character you can act out conversations in the mirror with. Apart from the discussion activities, all the other exercises are suitable for self-study as they stand.

IELTS Life Skills

CEFR Level: B1

8

theme-based
Preparation Sections

Section 1

Free-time Activities

Play – Do – Go

Exercise 1
Look at the pictures. Write the missing letters to complete the name of each activity. Use the prompt words.

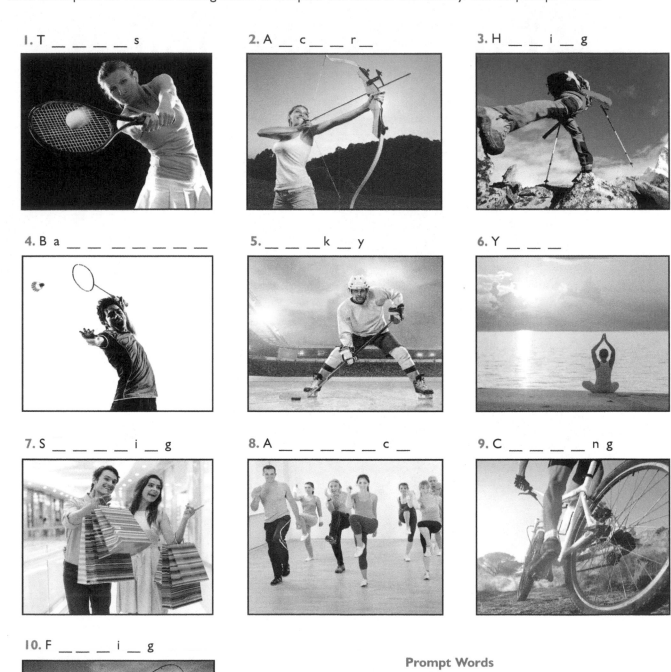

1. T _ _ _ _ s

2. A _ c _ _ r _

3. H _ _ i _ g

4. B a _ _ _ _ _ _ _ _

5. _ _ _ k _ y

6. Y _ _ _

7. S _ _ _ _ i _ g

8. A _ _ _ _ _ _ c _

9. C _ _ _ _ n g

10. F _ _ _ i _ g

Prompt Words

fishing	cricket	cycling
yoyo	tetris	acrobats
archery	shopping	finding
badminton	hiring	donkey
aikido	hockey	hiking
baseball	singing	yoga
aerobics	tennis	

Exercise 2

A. Match the activities in the box to the verbs.

Do	Play	Go

baseball	football
martial arts	hill walking
snowboarding	volleyball
puzzles	golf
swimming	skiing
pilates	surfing

B. Complete the table in **Exercise 2A** with the activities from **Exercise 1**, e.g. *do yoga*.

Exercise 3

Work in pairs. Discuss which activities above you like doing and which ones you dislike. Say why.

- What do you <u>like</u> do<u>ing</u>?

- I <u>like</u> play<u>ing</u> football. It's …

- What do you <u>enjoy</u> do<u>ing</u>?

- I <u>enjoy</u> go<u>ing</u> shopping. It's …

- I <u>dislike</u> go<u>ing</u> surfing because … What about you?

- Oh, no. I really <u>enjoy</u> go<u>ing</u> surfing. It's …

Used to

Exercise 1

Read the dialogue and answer the questions.

Mark: *Did you use to* do different things in your free time in Spain?

Roser: Yes, I did. For example, because the weather was much better than here in the UK, I *used to* have a lot of barbecues in the summer. I *used to* invite all my friends around. We *used to* have great house parties.

Mark: *Did you use to* go out dancing much? I hear the nightlife in Spain is awesome.

Roser: We *didn't use to* go to clubs very often. We *used to* hang out on the beach. Sometimes, we *used to* go camping there. We *used to* sit around the campfire singing and dancing together. What *did you use to* do in Holland?

Mark: Well, I *used to* be a big fan of heavy metal music, so I *used to* go to a lot of music festivals with my friends. We *used to* go camping too – at the festivals, you know?

Roser: Nice! But you say you *used to* be a big fan of heavy metal. Are you not anymore?

Mark: Not since I became a musician. After I learned to play the Spanish guitar, I became a big fan of classical music. That's all I listen to today!

A. We use **used to** to talk about things we did in the past that we *still do / don't do anymore*.

B. Complete the table with the correct forms of **used to**:

Used to	Example	Short Answer
Question	_____ you _____ play football in Spain?	✓ Yes, I _____ . ✗ No, I _____ .
Positive	Yes. I _____ play football every evening with my friends.	
Negative	No. I _____ play football at all when I lived there.	

Section 1

Exercise 2
A. Look at the pictures. Write the missing letters to complete each activity.

1. H _ _ e   a
   b _ r b _ c _ e

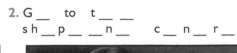

2. G _   to   t _ _
   s h _ p _ _ _ n _   c _ n _ r _

3. G _   to   m _ s _ _
   f _ s _ _ v _ l _

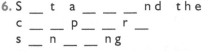

4. G _   c _ m _ _ ng

5. G _   to   t _ _
   c _ n _ m _

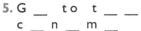

6. S _ _ t a _ _ _ _ nd   the
   c _ _ p _ _ r _
   s _ n _ _ ng

Prompt Words

shop, have, sing, go, sit
the, a
music, cinema, barbecue, centre, camping, festival, campfire
at, around, to

B. Work in pairs. Discuss what activities you used to and didn't use to do when you were younger.

Exercise 3
A. Put these activities in the order you like to do them. **1** = your favourite. **12** = your least favourite.

I prefer ...

read books	_____	surf the internet	_____	stream films and	
go to the gym	_____	go to museums		music videos	_____
sunbathe	_____	and art galleries	_____	play video games	_____
enjoy the outdoors	_____	use social networks	_____	cook meals	_____
listen to music	_____	watch TV	_____		

B. Work in pairs. Discuss which activities you prefer doing.

- Which do you prefer:
reading books or cooking meals?

- I prefer cooking meals to reading books.
I find reading boring.

- What about going to the gym or surfing the internet?
- I like them both the same. It's important to keep fit so I go to the gym a lot. Surfing the internet helps me to relax.

Please turn to page 46 now to start your exam practice.

Section 2

Weather

Hot and cold

Exercise 1

A. What's the temperature like? Write the words in the box in the correct order next to the thermometer.

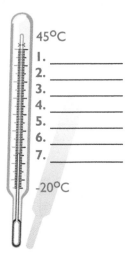

45°C

1. _____
2. _____
3. _____
4. _____
5. _____
6. _____
7. _____

-20°C

| boiling |
| cool |
| cold |
| freezing |
| hot |
| mild |
| warm |

B. What are the four seasons (**1-4**)? Write the missing letters.

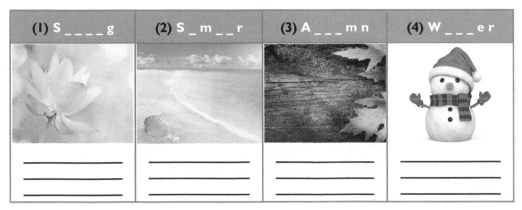

(1) S _ _ _ _ g	(2) S _ m _ _ r	(3) A _ _ _ m n	(4) W _ _ _ e r
‾‾‾‾‾‾	‾‾‾‾‾‾	‾‾‾‾‾‾	‾‾‾‾‾‾

C. Now write each word from **Exercise A** in the column (**1-4**) of the season it describes in your home country. There are no right answers.

D. Discuss these questions in pairs.

- What's the temperature like outside?

- It's freezing!

- What's it like here in summer?

- Here in Siberia, it's cold in summer.

- How about in winter?

- What was the temperature like last month?

- Last month, it was freezing!

Raining cats and dogs

Exercise 1

A. What's the weather like? Match the words to the types of weather in the pictures.

1. _____

2. _____

3. _____

4. _____

5. _____

6. _____

7. _____

8. _____

9. _____

10. _____

Prompt Words

snowing	thunder
raining	drizzle
sleety	foggy
hail	sunny
cloudy	windy

Section 2

B. Complete the table with the correct word forms.

Verb + ing	Noun	Adjective
snowing	snow	_____
_____	_____	rainy
_____	hail	
_____	_____	sleety
	cloud	_____
	_____	thundery
	sunshine	_____
_____	_____	drizzly
	fog	_____
	_____	windy
It is ... + ing.	There is	It is ... .

C. Choose the correct answer.

1. *It is / There is* snowing.
2. *It is / There is* sleety.
3. *It is / There is* thunder.
4. *It is / There is* foggy.
5. *It is / There is* sunshine.
6. *It is / There is* drizzling.

D. What's the weather like? Discuss these questions in pairs.

- What's the weather
like outside?

- It's cloudy. There's some
drizzle. But it's quite warm.

- What's it like
here in winter?

- It's usually cold and
there is snow.

- How about in
summer?

- What was the
weather like yesterday?

- It was cloudy and then
there was some rain.

- What's the
temperature like in
autumn in your
country?

- It is usually cool,
around 18ºC.

Section 2

Be going to – weather forecast

Exercise 1

Read the weather forecast and answer the questions.

> **Forecaster:** *What's the weather going to be like tomorrow? Well, it's going to be sunny in the morning. There aren't going to be any clouds in the sky. However, it's going to rain in the afternoon. It's also going to be very windy then. In the evening, there's going to be lots of sunshine. There are going to be a few showers too, but it isn't going to rain as much as in the afternoon.*

A. In the table, complete the Question with the correct form of *be going to*.

B. Choose the correct options to complete the rest of the table.

Be going to		Example
Question		What _____ the weather _____ _____ be like tomorrow?
Answer	**(for weather verbs)**	✓ It *'s going to be* / *'s going to* rain. ✗ It *'s not going to be* / *'s not going to* rain.
	(for weather adjectives)	✓ It *'s going to be* / *'s going to* rainy. ✗ It *'s not going to be* / *'s not going to* rainy.
	(for weather nouns)	✓ There *'s going to be* / *'s going to* rain. ✗ There *'s not going to be* / *'s not going to* rain. ✓ There *are going to be* / *are going to* showers. ✗ There *are not going to be* / *are not going to* showers.

C. Which word in the forecast means short periods of rain (rain ●◦ no rain ●◦ rain ●◦ no rain, etc.)? _____

D. Choose the correct answer.

   1. *It is going to be / There is going to be* snowing.   **2.** *It is going to be / There are going to be* sleety.

   3. *It is going to / There is going to be* thunder.   **4.** *It is going to be / It is going to* snow.

   5. *It is going to be / There is going to be* sunshine.   **6.** *It is going to be / It is going to* drizzle.

Exercise 2

A. Work in pairs, Student 1 and Student 2.

Student 1:   Turn to page 36. Look at the weather map for the UK. This is tomorrow's weather forecast. You are the forecaster. Present the forecast to Student 2.

                Here's the weather forecast for tomorrow. In London, it's going to be … . In Bournemouth, there's going to be …

Student 2:   Turn to page 37. Listen to Student 1 present the forecast and fill in the weather map.

B. Work in the same pairs, Student 1 and Student 2.

Student 2:   Turn to page 37. Look at the weather forecasts for London, Cardiff and Glasgow. This is tomorrow's weather forecast. You are the forecaster. Present the forecast to Student 1.

                Here's the weather forecast for London tomorrow. In the morning, it's going to be … .
                In the afternoon, there's going to be …

Student 1:   Turn to page 36. Listen to Student 2 present the forecast and fill in the weather table.

Please turn to page 48 now to start your exam practice.

Section 3

Holidays and leisure

Dream holidays!

Exercise 1

Unjumble (lebmjuun= unjumble) the words in red. Match the holiday types to the pictures.

1. nus _____ holiday

2. ytci _____ break

3. redaenvut _____ holiday

4. ctityavi _____ holiday

5. keendew _____ break

6. rifasa _____ holiday

7. ppngihso _____ break

8. ylfmai _____ holiday

9. ngimpac _____ holiday

10. aps _____ holiday

11. uicrse _____ holiday

12. wsno _____ holiday

Section 3

Exercise 2

Discuss these questions in pairs.

1. Which type of holiday in Exercise 1 would you prefer to go on?
2. Which type of holiday would you least like to go on?
3. What do you think a stay-at-home holiday is? Would you like to go on one of these?

> - Which type of holiday <u>would you prefer to</u> go on?
>
> - I <u>would prefer to</u> go on a sun holiday because I love to relax and sunbathe.

> - How about you?
>
> - I <u>would like to</u> go on a snow holiday because then I could try skiing for the first time.

Countryside versus city

Exercise 1

A. Which places and things in the box match to the city? Which match to the countryside? Write them in the circles. There are some words which match to both the city and the countryside.

Note: Use your dictionary to help you.

library	coast
museum	cave
scenery	theatre
wildlife	the underground
palace	cottage
sunset	skyscraper
castle	wood
waterfall	stream
stadium	river
farmland	pedestrian zone
cafe	village
department store	valley
gallery	harbour

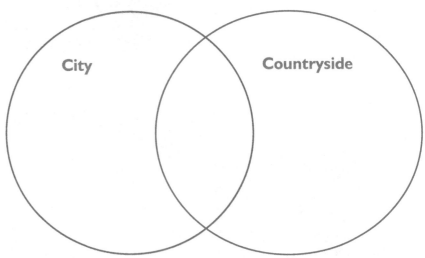

B. Which activities in the box match to the city? Which match to the countryside? Write them in the circles. There are some words which match to both the city and the countryside.

Note: Use your dictionary to help you.

going horse riding
going on an open-top bus tour
going fishing
going sightseeing
going hillwalking
visiting famous landmarks
going to an exhibition
going to a play
doing adventure sports
doing water sports
going to a musical
visiting Chinatown
doing snow sports
going mountain biking
visiting parliament
taking a tour of the castle
going on the big wheel
going to the amusements
visiting a theme park
seeing ancient sites

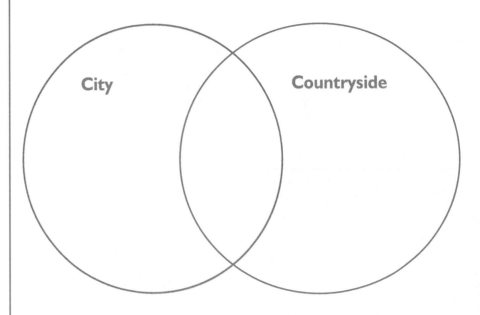

C. Complete the table of comparative adverbs.

Adjective	Comparative form
quiet	quieter
noisy	
exciting	more exciting
interesting	
friendly	
healthy	
dangerous	
popular	
safe	
boring	
big	
polluted	
beautiful	
clean	
modern	

D. Write sentences using the cue words in brackets.

1. The countryside is cleaner than the city.   *(city / countryside / clean)*

2. _____   *(city / countryside / polluted)*

3. _____   *(city / countryside / boring)*

4. _____   *(city / countryside / dangerous)*

5. _____   *(city / countryside / beautiful)*

6. _____   *(city / countryside / noisy)*

7. _____   *(city / countryside / modern)*

8. _____   *(city / countryside / friendly)*

E. Discuss these questions in pairs.

1. Which would you rather visit – the city or the countryside?

2. What would you rather do on holiday – go sightseeing or go to an exhibition?

3. Which is more exciting – going to the amusements or doing adventure sports? Why?

4. Which is more interesting – seeing ancient sites or going to a museum? Why?

- Which <u>would you rather</u> visit – the city or the countryside?

- I <u>would rather</u> visit the city <u>than</u> the countryside because …

- How about you?

- I <u>would prefer to</u> visit the countryside because …

- Which is more exiting – going to the amusements or doing adventure sports?

- I think doing adventure sports is <u>more exciting than</u> going to the amusements because …

The best memories!

Exercise 1

Complete the table with the superlative adjectives.

Adjective	Comparative form	Superlative Form
good	better	the best
bad	worse	
funny	funnier	
brave	braver	
amazing	more amazing	
unusual	more unusual	

Exercise 2

The present perfect

Read the interview and answer the questions.

Interviewer: What's the best place you've ever visited?

Sarah: Oh, that's a difficult question. The worst place I've ever visited is Seattle because it rained all the time I was there! The best? Um ... The best place I've ever visited is Iceland because the scenery there is beautiful.

Interviewer: Is it the most unusual place you've ever seen?

Sarah: Uh ... no, actually. Iceland's definitely the most beautiful place I've ever been to, but the most unusual place I've ever seen is *Glass Beach* in California. The sand on the beach is mostly made out of glass that was dumped there many years ago. I've never seen anything like it!

A. Complete the table with the correct present perfect forms.

The present perfect	Example	Short answer.
Question form	_____ you ever _____ a very unusual place?	✓ Yes, I _____ . ✗ No, I _____ .
Positive form (✓)	The most unusual place I _____ ever _____ is Scotland.	
Negative form (✗)	I _____ never _____ anywhere very unusual.	

B. Complete each question with the correct present perfect form of the verb in brackets.

1. What is the bravest thing you _____ ever _____ (*do*)?
2. What is the funniest thing that _____ ever _____ (*happen*) to you on holiday?
3. What is the most amazing holiday you _____ ever _____ (*have*)?
4. What is the most unusual place you _____ ever _____ (*visit*)?
5. What is the worst experience you _____ ever _____ (*have*) on holiday?

C. Work in pairs. Discuss the questions in **Exercise B**.

> - What's the bravest thing you've ever done?
> - The bravest thing I've ever done <u>is</u> present to a room full of people. I'm very shy and the first time I did it I was terrified!

Please turn to page 50 now to start your exam practice.

Section 4

Health

I feel ill

Exercise I

A. Look at the pictures. Write the missing letters to complete the name of each health problem.

I. B l _ _ d _ _ g

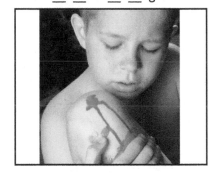

2. T _ _ p e _ a _ u _ e

3. B _ _ k e _ a _ m

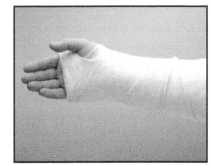

4. E _ r _ c h e

5. H _ _ d a _ _ _

6. B _ _ k _ _ _ e

7. S _ _ e t h _ _ _ t

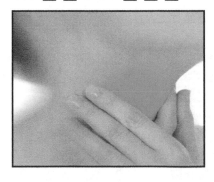

8. T _ _ t _ a c _ _

9. S _ _ m a _ h _ _ h e

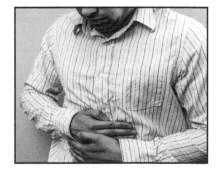

10. F _ v _ r

Prompt Words

temperature	earache
broken arm	fever
sore throat	bleeding
headache	toothache
stomach ache	backache

B. Match the advice to the definitions.

Advice	Definition
1. You must …	a. Do it.
2. You have to …	b. There's no need to do it.
3. You should …	c. Don't do it.
4. You don't have to …	d. It's a good idea to do it.
5. You mustn't …	e. Do it.

1. ....
2. ....
3. ....
4. ....
5. ....

C. Choose the correct answers.

1. **A.** I've got a temperature of 41.5° Celsius.
   B. You *should / must* go to the doctor.

2. **A.** I've got a sore throat.
   B. You *have to / should* suck some sweets.

3. **A.** I've got a really bad backache.
   B. You *mustn't / don't have to* lift heavy objects.

4. **A.** I've got a really bad fever. Could you stay with me a while?
   B. Of course. You *mustn't / don't have to* ask. I want to help. What can I do to make you more comfortable?

5. **A.** I've broken my arm. I can see the bone.
   B. You *have to / should* go to the hospital.

What should I do?

Exercise 1

Match the words to the 14 pictures.

accident	chemist's/pharmacy	operation
ambulance	cold	plaster
bandage	cough	swollen
bone	cut	tablet/pill/medicine
brain	fever	

1. _____

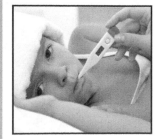

2. _____

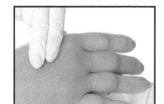

3. _____

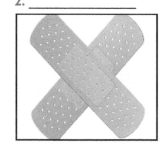

4. _____

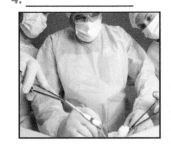

5. _____

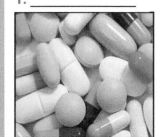

6. _____

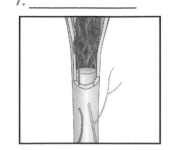

7. _____

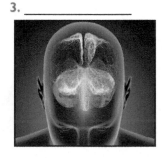

8. _____

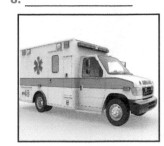

9. _____

10. _____

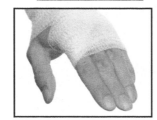

11. _____

12. _____

13. _____

14. _____

Exercise 2

A. Choose the correct option to complete each sentence.

1. **A.** I'm really tired and stressed after work.
   B. You should *get / make* some rest.

2. **A.** I've been feeling tired for about 6 months.
   B. You should *see / go* a doctor.

3. **A.** I've chipped my tooth.
   B. You must *get / go to* the dentist.

4. **A.** I've broken my hand.
   B. You must *get / go to* the A&E*.

5. **A.** I need some stronger pills.
   B. You have to *get / make* a prescription.

6. **A.** I'm here to see the doctor.
   B. I'm sorry. You must *get / make* an appointment.

7. **A.** I've got a pain in my heart.
   B. You must *call / get* an ambulance.

8. **A.** I feel really hot.
   B. You should *take / see* your temperature.

9. **A.** What is the situation, Doctor?
   B. You have to *do / have* an operation.

10. **A.** My leg is swollen.
    B. You should *put / take* some ice on it.

11. **A.** My head aches.
    B. If I were you I would *do / take* some pills.

12. **A.** I've cut myself.
    B. You should *put / make* a plaster on it.

*A&E = the Accident and Emergency department at a hospital

B. Work in pairs, Student 1 and Student 2. Explain the problem. Give advice.

1. Student 1: problem: cold
   Student 2: give advice

2. Student 2: problem: feel tired and sick
   Student 1: give advice

3. Student 1: problem: swollen ankle
   Student 2: give advice

4. Student 2: problem: small cut
   Student 1: give advice

- I've ... What should I do?

- If I were you, I would ... **or** ... I think you should ...

Please turn to page 52 now to start your exam practice.

Section 4

Section 5

Dinner party

First course

Exercise 1

Look at the pictures. Write the missing letters to complete the name of each starter.

1. _ _ _ h r _ _ m
   _ _ _ p

2. _ p _ n _ c _ and
   c _ e _ s _ _ _ e

3. _ _ t t _ c _ a _ d
   _ _ m _ t _ s _ l _ d

4. _ _ r l _ c
   _ _ e _ d

5. _ _ l _ n

6. _ _ e e _ e
   _ _ a _ k _

Prompt Words

cheese snacks	melon
spinach and cheese pie	garlic bread
lettuce and tomato salad	mushroom soup

Exercise 2

Question Tags

Mark and Emma are going to have a dinner party. Read their conversation and complete the question tags.

Mark: Emma, we won't order takeaway, (1) __*will*__ we?

Emma: Oh, no. Let's cook our own food, (2) _____ we?

Mark: Yes, OK. Garlic bread would be good for starters, (3) _____ it?

Emma: Yes, it would; especially for vegetarians. It's a good idea to have more than one starter, though, (4) _____ it?

Mark: Yes, it is. Duck in plum sauce sounds nice, (5) _____ it?

Emma: Oh, yes it really does. OK, then. We're happy with our starters, (6) _____ we?

Mark: Yes, we are. Let me write that down. So it was garlic bread and duck in plum sauce, (7) _____ it?

Emma: Yes, it was. We should pick two things for each course, (8) _____ we?

Mark: Yes, we should. Let's have one vegetarian option and one meat option.

Second course

Exercise 1

Complete the menu. Use the clues to help you.

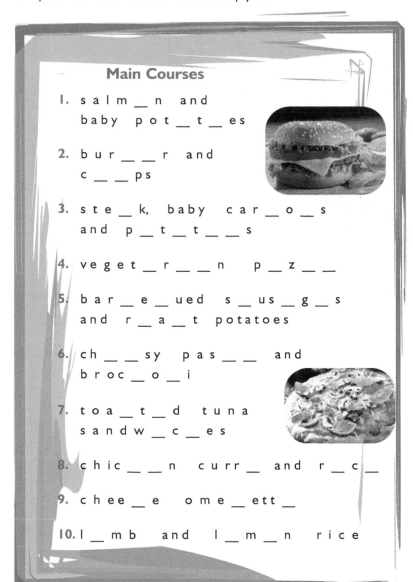

Main Courses

1. s a l m __ n and
   b a b y p o t __ t __ e s

2. b u r __ __ r a n d
   c __ __ p s

3. s t e __ k, b a b y c a r __ o __ s
   a n d p __ t __ t __ __ s

4. v e g e t __ r __ __ n p __ z __ __

5. b a r __ e __ u e d s __ u s __ g __ s
   a n d r __ a __ t p o t a t o e s

6. c h __ __ s y p a s __ __ a n d
   b r o c __ o __ i

7. t o a __ t __ d t u n a
   s a n d w __ c __ e s

8. c h i c __ __ __ n c u r r __ a n d r __ c __

9. c h e e __ e o m e __ e t t __

10. l __ m b a n d l __ m __ n r i c e

Clues

1. a type of fish; a round vegetable

2. meat in bread; fries in the USA

3. a big piece of meat; they're orange; they're round

4. no meat; Italian favourite

5. cooked outside; a long piece of meat; a type of cooking – boiled, fried, etc.

6. a dairy product; Italian food; green vegetable

7. cooked in a toaster; a fish; bread on both sides

8. white meat; Indian food – hot; sounds like spice

9. from a cow; cooked in a frying pan – French food

10. a baby sheep; sounds like spice

Exercise 2

Read some more of Mark and Emma's conversation. Then answer the questions.

Mark: OK, so … what about the main course?

Emma: Well, I think we should have a simple vegetarian dish like vegetarian pizza. *What do you think?*

Mark: Good idea. *How about a fish dish as well?*

Emma: Yeah. *Why don't we have salmon and baby potatoes?*

Mark: Great idea! *What about a meat dish too?*

Emma: Yeah, you're right. Not everyone likes fish. Maybe we need a third main course. *Have you got any suggestions?*

Mark: I think another simple dish like burger and chips is best. After all, we've got to do all the cooking! *Does that sound OK?*

Emma: Yeah. Perfect!

A. Which questions in *green* are actually suggestions? Write them here:

_____

_____

_____

_____

B Which questions in *green* are real questions (asking for an opinion, not offering suggestion)? Write them here:

_____

_____

_____

_____

Section 5

21

Third course

Exercise 1
Match the words to the pictures.

cheesecake	coconut cream pie	ice cream
chocolate cookies	fruit salad	strawberry yoghurt

1. _____

2. _____

3. _____

4. _____

5. _____

6. _____

Exercise 2
Read more of Mark and Emma's conversation and choose the correct options.

Mark: Now, how about dessert? I think we **(1)** *should / shall* choose two different desserts. No more than that because it's a lot of work, right?

Emma: I agree. **(2)** *Lets / Let's* pick two simple popular dishes. Cheesecake sounds nice, **(3)** *isn't / doesn't* it?

Mark: Yum! And what about a healthy option like fruit salad? That would be popular too, **(4)** *would / wouldn't* it?

Emma: Yeah. Sounds perfect!

Your dinner party

Exercise 1
A. Now work in pairs. You are going to have a dinner party. Make suggestions on what food to cook and agree on the first, second and third courses of your menu.

- For the first course, <u>why don't we</u> … ?

- Good idea. Let's … What do you think?

- <u>I think we should</u> … .

- OK. And <u>how about</u> … ?

B. Write your finished menu here.

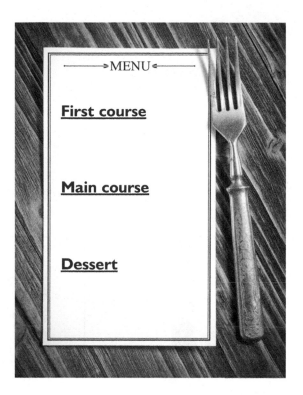

→MENU←

First course

Main course

Dessert

Shopping list

Exercise 1

A. Mark and Emma are deciding what they need to buy. Choose the correct options to complete the conversation.

Mark: OK. Let's look at what we need to buy. Have we got **(1)** *any / some* plums?

Emma: No, we haven't. Put them on the shopping list. We only need **(2)** *a few / few*, though. Don't get too **(3)** *much / many*. Six or so should be fine.

Mark: OK. Six plums. How about duck? I think we have **(4)** *some / any*. And we're OK for bread and garlic too. Although we need **(5)** *some / a* butter.

Emma: Yeah. You're right. We're OK for duck, etc.,

but need butter. And we've got **(6)** *none / no* pizza bases for the vegetarian pizza. We also need **(7)** *lots of / much* vegetables for the topping. We haven't got **(8)** *much / many* cheese either. Let's get **(9)** *some / any* more.

Mark: OK. Pizza bases, vegetables, cheese – all on the list. We've got plenty of burgers, chips, salmon and potatoes, so the rest of the main courses are OK. I don't think we've got **(10)** *many / much* fruit, though, for the salad. Let's get **(11)** *a / some* bunch of bananas and **(12)** *a / some* grapes. We've got all the ingredients we need for the cheesecake, though.

B. Work in pairs. Make a shopping list of things you need to buy for your dinner party.

C. What about drinks? Write the missing letters to complete the drink names.

1. C _ f _ e _   ☐
2. T _ _   ☐
3. S _ _ t d _ _ n k _   ☐
4. W _ _ e   ☐
5. B _ _ r   ☐
6. L _ m _ n _ d _   ☐

D. Work in pairs. What drinks do you want for your party? Discuss and tick the drinks in **Exercise C** that you will use.

Please turn to page 54 now to start your exam practice.

Section 6

Transport

How I get there

Exercise 1
A. Complete the phrases.

Travel...

1. by   c _ r

2. on   f _ _ t

3. by   t _ _ m

4. by   t _ x _

5. by   t _ a _ n

6. by   f _ r _ y

7. by   c _ _ ch

8. by   b _ _

9. on   the
   u _ d _ _ _ g _ _ u _ d

10. by   b _ _ e

B. Choose the correct options.

1. go / take **a taxi**
2. get *a* / *the* **bus**
3. get *a* / *the* **train**
4. *go* / *take* **on the underground**

C. Write the words in the box in the correct order on the line.

| occasionally |
| often |
| rarely |
| sometimes |
| usually |

Never, _____, _____, _____,

_____, _____, Always

D. Work in pairs. Say how often you travel by the different methods in **Exercise A**.

- I often travel by car to work. How about you?

- I never travel by car to work. I always cycle there.

- I sometimes get the bus into the city centre at weekends. You?

- Um … I rarely get the bus into town. I usually go on the underground.

By road

Exercise 1
A. How often do you do these things?

1. hitchhike — Always / Usually / Often / Sometimes / Occasionally / Rarely / Never
2. speed when I'm driving — Always / Usually / Often / Sometimes / Occasionally / Rarely / Never
3. ignore traffic lights — Always / Usually / Often / Sometimes / Occasionally / Rarely / Never
4. make long journeys — Always / Usually / Often / Sometimes / Occasionally / Rarely / Never
5. ignore traffic policeman — Always / Usually / Often / Sometimes / Occasionally / Rarely / Never
6. drive safely — Always / Usually / Often / Sometimes / Occasionally / Rarely / Never
7. get the bus to work/college — Always / Usually / Often / Sometimes / Occasionally / Rarely / Never
8. cycle places — Always / Usually / Often / Sometimes / Occasionally / Rarely / Never
9. walk to the shops — Always / Usually / Often / Sometimes / Occasionally / Rarely / Never
10. drive on motorways — Always / Usually / Often / Sometimes / Occasionally / Rarely / Never
11. drive a scooter — Always / Usually / Often / Sometimes / Occasionally / Rarely / Never
12. get a lift to work/college — Always / Usually / Often / Sometimes / Occasionally / Rarely / Never
13. drive in foreign countries — Always / Usually / Often / Sometimes / Occasionally / Rarely / Never
14. park in 'no parking' areas — Always / Usually / Often / Sometimes / Occasionally / Rarely / Never

B. Match the words in **Column A** to the phrases with the same meaning in **Column B**.

Column A	Column B
1. always	a. some of the time
2. usually	b. all of the time
3. often	c. most of the time
4. sometimes	d. a lot

1. ......
2. ......
3. ......
4. ......

Section 6

Section 6

C. Put a tick where the word/phrase in brackets should go in the sentence.

1. I ☐ hitchhike ☐. I think I did it once. *(rarely)*
2. I ☐ get the bus to college ☐.   *(all of the time)*
3. I ☐ get a lift to work ☐.   *(a lot)*
4. I ☐ drive safely ☐.   *(always)*
5. I ☐ make long journeys ☐.   *(some of the time)*
6. I ☐ walk to the shops ☐.   *(most of the time)*

D. Work in pairs. Say how often you do the things in **Exercise A.**

> - I never hitchhike. I think it's dangerous. How about you?
>
> - I rarely do it. I think I did it once.

> - I get the bus to college most of the time. How about you?
>
> - I rarely get the bus to college. I usually get a lift with my friend.

By plane

Exercise 1
A. How often do you do these things? Write *Always / Often / Usually / Sometimes / Rarely / Never*.

1. fly to foreign countries _____
2. use a cheap airline _____
3. go to the gate early _____
4. print out your boarding pass before you go to the airport _____
5. need a visa to travel _____
6. use different currencies _____
7. get sick on board the plane _____
8. feel nervous during take-off _____
9. shop in the duty-free _____
10. only take hand luggage _____
11. bring check-in baggage _____
12. arrive late for check-in _____

B. Work in pairs. Compare your and your partner's answers.

The same answers	Different answers
… and … too.	… whereas …
… and … as well.	… but …

> I always feel nervous during take-off <u>and</u> you do <u>too</u>.

> I often get sick on board <u>whereas</u> you never do.

Make predictions

Exercise 1
A. Have a look at these pictures and choose the correct probability.

1. *probably / definitely* cancelled
2. *probably / definitely* related
3. *probably / definitely* friends
4. *probably / definitely* not moving
5. *probably / definitely* not in time for the bus

B. Match the probabilities to the percentages.

Percentage	Probability
1. 100%	a. Probably
2. 75%	b. Probably not
3. 50%	c. Definitely
4. 25%	d. Maybe
5. 0%	e. Definitely not

1. ....
2. ....
3. ....
4. ....
5. ....

C. Choose the correct options to complete the predictions.

1. *Probably I'll / I'll probably* visit London next year.
2. *Definitely I'll / I'll definitely* go on the London Eye if I do.
3. *Maybe I'll / I'll maybe* watch a musical in the West End.
4. *I'll not definitely / I definitely won't / Definitely I'll not* forget to visit my aunt there.
5. *She'll not probably / She probably won't / Probably she'll not* recognise me – it's been six years since I last saw her!

D. Choose the correct options to complete the grammar table.

Form	Example	Short Answer
Question	Will you ever *travel / to travel* to Latin America?	✔ Yes, *I'll / I will*. ✗ No, *I will not / I won't*.
Positive sentence	I'll definitely *to travel / travel* to Latin America one day.	
Negative sentence	I definitely *not to travel / won't travel* there.	

E. Work in pairs. Make predictions about what's going to happen next in each scene.

Scene 1	Scene 2	Scene 3	Scene 4

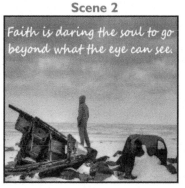

Exercise 2

A. Match the phrases of similar meaning.

Column A	Column B
1. I'll definitely ...	a. I'm sure I'll ...
2. I'll probably ...	b. I may / I might ...
3. Maybe I'll ...	c. I don't think I'll ...
4. I probably won't ...	d. I'm certain I won't ...
5. I definitely won't ...	e. I think I'll ...

1. ......
2. ......
3. ......
4. ......
5. ......

B. Work in pairs. Ask and answer the questions.

1. Do you think you'll ever travel to America in the future?
2. Will you cycle more in the future?
3. Do you think public transport will improve in the future?
   - Will there be fewer delays?
   - Will buses and trains be less crowded?
   - Will buses and trains be safer?
   - Will they be faster?
   - Will more people use them instead of cars?
4. Do you think you'll ever travel to space?

Please turn to page 56 now to start your exam practice.

Section 7

My family - My home

Who's who

Exercise I

A. Look at the family tree. Complete the sentences using the words in the box.

wife	grandad	daughter	great-grandad	niece	sister
husband	mother	father	uncle	aunt	brother
married	son	grandma	nephew	great-grandson	cousin

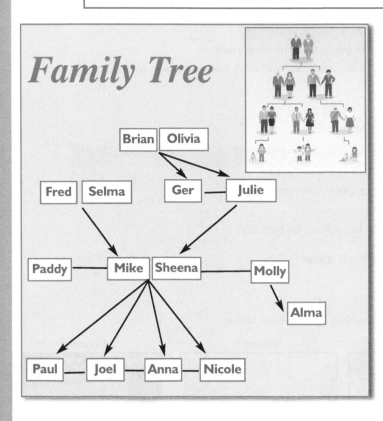

Family Tree

1. Olivia's _____ is called Joel.
2. Joel's _____ is called Brian.
3. Brian's _____ is called Olivia.
4. Brian is _____ to Olivia.
5. Olivia's _____ is called Brian.
6. Joel's _____ is called Mike.
7. Joel's _____ is called Sheena.
8. Sheena's _____s are called Anna and Nicole.
9. Joel's _____ is called Nicole.
10. Paul's _____ is called Joel.
11. Joel's _____ is called Molly.
12. Paddy's _____ is called Joel.
13. Molly's _____ is called Anna.
14. Joel's _____ is called Paddy.
15. Joel's _____ is called Selma.
16. Joel's _____ is called Fred.
17. Mike's got two _____s called Joel and Paul.
18. Joel's _____ is called Alma.

B. Work in pairs. Look at the pictures below. Decide which member of Joel's family you think each one is.

You're certain:	"That **must be** Joel's sister. The picture's very modern."
You think it's possible:	"That **could/might be** Joel's mum. The picture's quite old."
You think it's not possible:	"It **mustn't be** Joel's dad because the picture looks too old."
You're certain it isn't:	"That **can't be** Joel's brother – it's a baby girl."

1. _____   2. _____   3. _____   4. _____   5. _____

Exercise 2

A. Draw your own family tree. Then work in pairs and introduce your family to your partner.

My family tree

> I'm married to Brian. We've got two sons called Tom and Dave and one daughter called Tracy.

> I've got two sisters, Nicki and Kate. Kate's the eldest. I'm the youngest. Nicki's in the middle.

B. Match the adjectives to their meanings.

Adjective	Meaning	
1. reliable	a. You want to hear what they have to say.	1. ......
2. negative	b. They have a lot of belief in themselves.	2. ......
3. positive / cheerful	c. They always think bad things will happen.	3. ......
4. rude	d. They are a little bit mad. They do unusual things.	4. ......
5. polite	e. They get good grades.	5. ......
6. serious	f. They always say hello and like to chat.	6. ......
7. nervous	g. They believe things should be done the way they were in the past.	7. ......
8. friendly	h. Everyone likes them. They make a good impression on people.	8. ......
9. fun-loving	i. They never get very worried or angry. They stay relaxed.	9. ......
10. funny	j. They tell really good jokes.	10. ......
11. clever	k. They don't laugh or tell jokes often.	11. ......
12. patient	l. They never say *please* and *thank you* and they are not nice to older people.	12. ......
13. calm	m. They always expect good things to happen.	13. ......
14. charming	n. They can wait a long time to get what they want. They don't mind if things take a long time to do.	14. ......
15. confident	o. You know if you ask them to do something, they will do it. You can trust them.	15. ......
16. crazy	p. They always say *please* and *thank you* and they respect other people.	16. ......
17. cruel	q. They worry about what will happen a lot.	17. ......
18. quiet / shy	r. They enjoy laughing and having a good time.	18. ......
19. old-fashioned	s. They do not like to be around lots of loud people.	19. ......
20. interesting	t. They are mean to people.	20. ......

C. Find the opposites of these words in **Exercise B**.

1. Shy _____

2. Funny _____

3. Positive _____

4. Polite _____

5. Nervous _____

D. Organise the words in **Exercise B** into good and bad characteristics.

Good characteristics	Bad characteristics

E. Work in pairs. Ask and answer these questions.

1. Is being shy a good or bad character trait? Maybe it's neither! Look at both sides.

> On one hand, ...   On the other hand, ...

2. Think of a friend or family member you admire. Describe their character. Explain with examples.

> I really admire my friend Jean because she is so confident. For example, last week she had to give a speech in front of all our bosses at work. Jean got up and spoke without any notes.

3. Think of a famous person you admire. Say why. Link your ideas together.

> I really admire ... because (s)he is ... .   For example, ... And another thing I admire about her/him is ... . For example ... .   She/He's also ... .   For instance, ...

My home

Exercise 1

A. Write the missing letters to complete the words.

Rooms

1. b __ d __ __ __ __ m

2. b __ __ __ r __ __ __

3. k __ __ c h __ __

4. l __ __ n __ e

5. s __ t t __ __ __
   r __ __ m

6. d __ __ i n g
   __ __ __ m

7. h __ __ l

8. c e __ l __ r

Features

1. b a l c _ _ _ y

2. g a r _ g _

3. b a _ _ h t _ b

4. g a r _ _ _ n

5. p r i v _ _ t _ _
p _ _ r _ _ _ n g

6. c o n s _ _ r v _ _ t _ _ r y

7. s u p e r f a s t
b _ _ o a _ b a _ _ _

8. e l e c _ _ r _ c
s _ _ o _ _ e r

9. en-suite
b _ _ _ h _ _ _ _ m

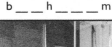

Appliances

1. w _ _ s h _ _ _ g
m _ c _ i n _

2. m i c _ _ o w _ _ _ e

3. d _ s _ w _ s _ _ _ r

4. t _ l _ v _ _ _ i o _

5. o _ _ _ n

6. f r _ d _ _ _

7. f _ e _ z _ r

8. d _ _ y _ r

9. a i r
c _ n _ _ t _ _ n _ _ g

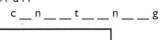

B. Answer the questionnaire for you. Tick the correct boxes.

Your Living Situation

1. What kind of accommodation are you living in?
   Flat ☐   House ☐

2. Does it have an upstairs and a downstairs or is it all on just one floor?
   One floor ☐   Two floors ☐

3. Are you renting or do you own your own place?
   Rent ☐   Own ☐

4. What's the neighbourhood you live in like?
   Noisy ☐   Quiet ☐
   Safe ☐   Dangerous ☐
   Good transport links ☐   Bad transport links ☐
   Good local facilities ☐   Bad local facilities ☐

5. Do you live near any of the following?
   Park ☐   Shopping centre ☐
   Pub ☐   Restaurants ☐
   Health centre ☐   Gym ☐
   Bus stop ☐   Train station ☐

C. Work in pairs, **Student 1** and **Student 2**.

Student 1: Turn to page 38 and follow the instructions.
Student 2: Turn to page 39 and follow the instructions.

D. Work in pairs, **Student 1** and **Student 2**.

Student 1: Turn to page 38 and follow the instructions.
Student 2: Turn to page 39 and follow the instructions

E. Work in pairs. Tell your partner about your home and neighbourhood. Say:

1. If you're renting or if you own your place.

2. What kind of place you live in (describe it – number of rooms, features, appliances, etc.).

3. What your neighbourhood is like (the good and bad things about it).

Please turn to page 58 now to start your exam practice.

Section 7

Section 8

Education and work

Back to school!

Exercise 1

A. Put the levels of English in the box in the right
   order: (1 = lowest; 4 = highest).

elementary	1. _____ level ☐
advanced	2. _____ level ☐
beginner	3. _____ level ☐
intermediate	4. _____ level ☐

B. Tick ✔ your current level of English.

C. *For* and *Since*
   How long have you been learning English?
   Choose the correct option to complete the sentences.

   1. I have been learning English *for / since* 2012.
   2. I have been learning English *for / since* 3 years.

D. *The present perfect continuous*
   Work in pairs. Discuss these questions:

> - How long <u>have you been</u> learn<u>ing</u> English?
>
> - I'<u>ve been</u> learn<u>ing</u> English for ...

1. How long have you been learning English?

2. Have you been doing much study for the IELTS exam?

3. Have you been watching English language programmes
   or films?

4. What other things have you been doing to prepare for
   the exam?

Exercise 2

A. Put the steps in order.

| higher education (university) | nursery school | secondary school | primary school |

1. _____ ➻ 2. _____ ➻ 3. _____ ➻ 4. _____

B. Match the words to the pictures.

| facilities | staff | equipment | pupils |

1. _____   2. _____   3. _____   4. _____

C. Put each thing in the box in the correct column – **Equipment** or **Facilities**.

sports field	computer lab	good lighting	comfortable desks and
whiteboards	Wi-Fi service	science lab	chairs
changing rooms	laptops	gym	superfast broadband
tablets	study rooms	spacious classrooms	service
canteen	projectors	air conditioning	
PCs	library	clean toilets & showers	

Equipment	Facilities

D. Work in pairs. Think about staff, pupils, facilities and equipment. Ask and answer the questions.

1. Think back to when you were at school. What was it like? How was it different to school today?
2. Are pupils respectful enough of teachers today? Do they behave well?
3. What needs to be done in order to make the education system better for learners?
4. Are pupils under more stress at school today than in the past? Why? / Why not?

Opinion Phrases
Here are some ways to introduce your opinion:

> The way I see it …   As far as I'm concerned …
> If you ask me …   As I see it …
> To my mind …   I believe …

Jobs

Exercise 1

A. Write the missing letters to complete the names of different jobs.

1. b _ t _ h _ _ _

2. d _ n _ _ _ _ t

3. s _ _ _ d _ _ _ r

4. d _ _ r _ c _ _ _ r

5. f _ _ _ m
s _ _ _ r

6. j _ _ _ rn _ l _ _ _ t

7. j _ d _ e

8. m _ c _ _ _ n _ _

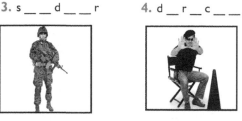

9. m _ d _ l

10. p h o t _ g _ _ _ ph _ r

11. t e _ _ n _ s
p _ _ a y _ r

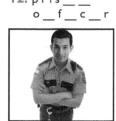

12. p r i s _ _ _
o _ f _ c _ r

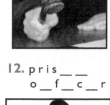

13. s e c _ r _ t _
g u a _ d

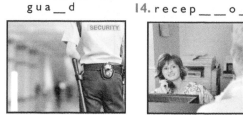

14. r e c e p _ _ _ o _ i s _

15. n _ r _ _ _

B. Think about the following questions and write one job on each answer line.

Which of the jobs in **Exercise A** do you think is …

1. … the most dangerous? _____
2. … the easiest? _____
3. … the hardest? _____
4. … the safest? _____
5. … the best paid? _____
6. … the most stressful? _____
7. … the one where you spend the longest hours at work each day? _____
8. … the lowest paid? _____

C. Work in pairs. Compare your answers to **Exercise B** and explain your choices.

> I think … is the easiest job for a number of reasons.
>
> First of all, …
>
> Secondly, …
>
> Furthermore, …

What if …

Exercise 1
A. Read about Michelle and then answer the questions.

Michelle

Then

Now

When I first arrived in Manchester, I was afraid and lonely. I couldn't communicate with anyone. My school had a special language programme to help kids like me learn English. *If I hadn't been part of that programme, life would have been very difficult.* Soon, I was learning lots of new words and, more importantly, I met other people in my situation – I made my first friends. Our teacher, Maria, was amazing – so kind and patient. *If I ever see her again, I will say a big thank you.* She helped change my life. After six months, my English had got much better so I left the programme and joined normal classes at the school. It still wasn't easy, but my English improved every day and slowly I became more fluent. It took about two years before I felt really confident, though. Then my grades in other subjects got better too – much better; I was top of my class. I did well enough in my A levels to study medicine at university. And that's where I'm at now – in my fourth year of a seven-year degree. Do I ever think about home? Of course. All the time. *If I'm upset, that's usually why.* But I'm also very happy here in the UK – my second home. It's given me lots of great opportunities. *If (or when!) I qualify as I doctor, I will go back to Uganda and volunteer there.* Few people there get the chance I've had. *If you are in a similar situation to 12-year-old, like I was, don't give up.* It's definitely not easy to learn a new language. But, *if I were you, I would keep trying.* And always have hope.

1. Being part of the language programme made life more difficult for Michelle.   *TRUE / FALSE*
2. Michelle has seen her old teacher, Maria, again since she left the programme and thanked her. *TRUE / FALSE*
3. Michelle is not twelve years old now.   *TRUE / FALSE*
4. Michelle does some volunteer work in Uganda whenever she can.   *TRUE / FALSE*

B. Put each sentence in *green* in the text in **Exercise A** in the correct column of the table.

Type	0 Conditional	1st Conditional	2nd Conditional	3rd Conditional
Examples:	*If I'm upset, that's usually why.*			

C. Choose the correct answers to complete the discussion.

Matt: *If you **worked** / **work** hard, do you always **got** / **get** rewarded?*

Rick: No, I don't think that's true. Some people who work very hard are poor their whole lives. Wouldn't you agree?

Matt: Yeah, definitely. *If you **moved** / **move** to the UK, **did** / **will** you live there forever?*

Rick: Um … No, I think I'll **returned** / **return** home in a few years. Home is where your heart is, right?

Matt: I don't know. I think I might stay in Britain the rest of my life. *If you **are** / **were** rich, would you still **study** / **studied** English?*

Rick: Uh … I guess so. … Yes, because it's a language I **could use** / **use** on my travels. After all, if I were rich, I **could travel** / **can travel** the globe! And you?

Matt: Yes, I **will** / **would**. I **still wanted** / **would still want** to live in Britain, you see. And if I were rich, I **could** / **can** buy a mansion there!

Rick: *If you **have** / **had** been born in an English-speaking country, would things have been easier for you?*

Matt: Hmm. Good question. In some ways they **have been** / **would have been**. I wouldn't **have** / **have had** to learn English as a second language, of course. On the other hand, maybe I **will** / **would** have got lazy and not tried to learn any foreign languages, you know?

Rick: Sure. If I **have been** / **had been** a native English speaker, I **might not try** / **might not have tried** to learn a second language either.

D. Work in pairs. Ask and answer the questions in *green* from **Exercise C**.

Have you got the right qualifications?

Exercise 1

A. Work in pairs, Student 1 and Student 2.

Student 1, turn to page 40 and follow the instructions.
Student 2, turn to page 42 and follow the instructions.

B. Rewrite 1-5 as polite questions/requests.

1. What qualifications have you got?
   Could you please tell me _____ have got?

2. Do you speak any foreign languages?
   Would you please tell me if _____ languages?

3. Where have you worked in the past?
   I would also like to know where_____ in the past.

4. Have you got any other relevant experience?
   Can you also tell me about _____ have got?

5. What are your personal qualities?
   I would like to know what your _____.

C. Work in the same pairs, Student 1 and Student 2.

Student 1, good news! Your application was accepted by Job4U Recruitment and they passed it on to an employer called RodCivil Eng. The owner of RodCivil, Rod Donal, liked your CV and has called you for interview. Begin the interview when Student 2 starts. Answer the factual questions using the information in the form you filled in in **Exercise 1A**. Answer the other questions with your own ideas.

Student 2, you are an employer called Rod Donal. You are going to interview Student 1 for a job. First, greet Student 1 politely. Then, ask him/her the questions in **Exercise 1B** and one question of your own. Start the interview when you are ready.

D. Work in the same pairs, Student 1 and Student 2.

Student 2, good news! Your application was accepted by Job4U Recruitment and they passed it on to an employer called Ash Teaching. The owner of Ash Teaching, Ashling Marie, liked your CV and has called you for interview. Begin the interview when Student 1 starts. Answer the factual questions using the information in the form you filled in in **Exercise 1A**. Answer the other questions with your own ideas.

Student 1, you are an employer called Ashling Marie. You are going to interview Student 2 for a job. First, greet Student 2 politely. Then, ask him/her the questions in **Exercise 1B** and one question of your own. Start the interview when you are ready.

Please turn to page 60 now to start your exam practice.

Section 8

35

Preparation Sections: Additional Material

Additional Material

Section 2

Exercise 2A

Student 1: Look at the weather map for the UK. This is tomorrow's weather forecast. You are the forecaster. Present the forecast to Student 2.

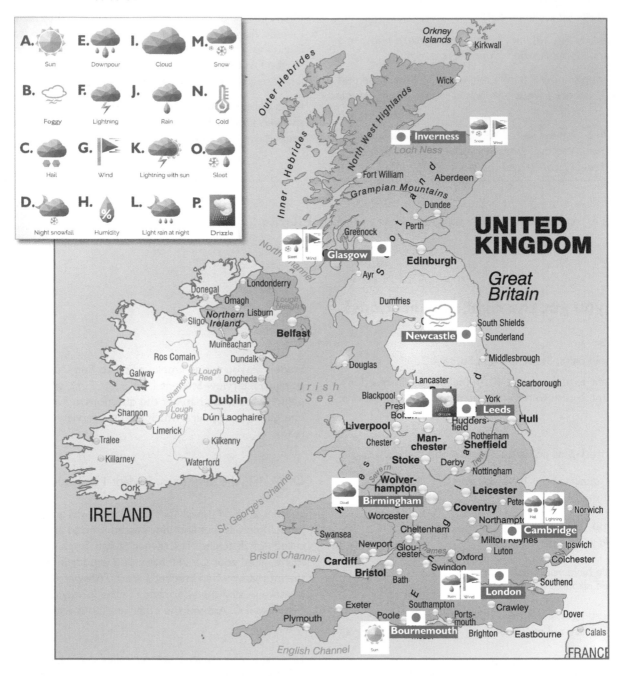

Exercise 2B

Student 1: Listen to Student 2 present the forecast and fill in the weather table.

	Morning	Afternoon	Evening
London			
Cardiff			
Glasgow			

Section 2

Exercise 2A
Student 2: Listen to Student 1 present the forecast and fill in the weather map.

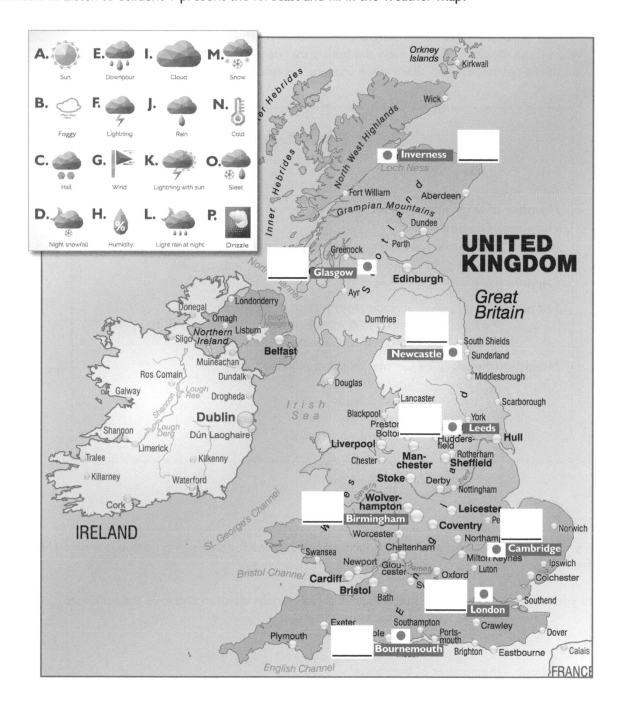

Exercise 2B
Student 2: Look at the weather forecasts for London, Cardiff and Glasgow. This is tomorrow's weather forecast. You are the forecaster. Present the forecast to Student 1.

	Morning	Afternoon	Evening
London	☀ 🚩	cloud/rain	cloud
Cardiff	cloud	☀	cloud 🚩
Glasgow	cloud ⚡	sleet	🚩

Additional Material

Section 7

Exercise 1C

Student 1: You're an estate agent (you sell houses). Student 2 rings you up to ask about a house. Answer Student 2's questions using the information on the card. Then, tell Student 2 why he/she should come and view the house; mention its good features and nice things about the neighbourhood. Start when Student 2 is ready. He/she rings, you answer.

Flat 8, Down Street

Price: £450,000
Basic Info:
Number of bedrooms: 2 [one is en-suite]
Number of bathrooms: 2
Kitchen appliances: washing machine, dryer, dish washer, fridge-freezer, oven
Parking: park on public road
Garden: front – no; back – yes

Features:	- Spacious rooms with high ceilings
	- Balcony off main bedroom – nice views of the park
	- Bath tub and an electric shower

Neighbourhood:	- Corner shop five minutes away
	- Very safe area
	- Good schools
	- Friendly neighbours
	- Good transport links

Exercise 1D

Student 1, you want to buy a new home for your family. You saw a for sale sign on a house and you like the look of it. Ring the estate agent (Student 2) and do the following:

1. Introduce yourself: - You and your husband have three teenage children and love the outdoors.
   - You are interested in Shepherd House, The Valley.
   - You want to find out more information.

2. Ask questions about: - the number of bedrooms
   - the number of bathrooms
   - the kitchen appliances

3. Ask the estate agent for any other information they have.

Note:

Be polite! Use the following phrases: Could you please tell me...? or Could you please let me know...? or I would be interested in knowing...

Section 7

Exercise 1C

Student 2, you want to buy a new home for your young family. You saw a for sale sign on a flat and you like the look of it. Ring the estate agent (Student 1) and do the following:

1. Introduce yourself: - You and your husband have one young child.
                         - You are interested in Flat 8, Downs Road.
                         - You want to find out more information.
2. Ask questions about: - the number of bedrooms
                         - the number of bathrooms
                         - the kitchen appliances
3. Ask the estate agent for any other information they have.

Note:

Be polite! Use the following phrases: Could you please tell me...? **or** *Could you please let me know...?* **or** *I would be interested in knowing...*

Exercise 1D

Student 1: You're an estate agent (you sell houses). Student 1 rings you up to ask about a house. Answer Student 1's questions using the information on the card. Then, tell Student 1 why he/she should come and view the house; mention its good features and nice things about the neighbourhood. Start when Student 1 is ready. He/she rings, you answer.

Shepherd House, The Valley

Price: £850,000
Basic Info:
Number of bedrooms: 4 [two are en-suite]
Number of bathrooms: 2
Kitchen appliances: washing machine, dryer, dish washer, fridge-freezer, oven, microwave
Parking: garage holds four cars
Garden: front and back

Features: - Spacious rooms with high ceilings
                       - Balconies off every bedroom with views of mountains
                       - Swimming pool and sauna

Neighbourhood: - Quiet, peaceful area
                       - No neighbours – very private
                       - School 15 minutes away
                       - Bus stop outside gate
                       - Four miles to outdoor sports centre

Section 8

Have you got the right qualifications?

Exercise 1

A. Student 1 read Stevie's career profile and use it to complete the Job4U Recruitment form that follows. Later, you will be Stevie so get to know him/her well!

Hi! My name's Stevie – Stevie Knowles. I'm originally from Ukraine, but I live here in London now – Flat 8, Malden Way, Shoreditch. I'm 29 years old.

Needless to say, I speak fluent Ukrainian. I also speak English to working proficiency level. My Russian is reasonably good, too. I'd rate myself as advanced.

Presently, I'm working as a Site Engineer for Rowan Construction. The role involves managing the engineering side of activity on different construction sites. Our building projects are mainly commercial, so I'm involved in building shopping centres and office blocks. I moved to the UK to take up this position. Before that, I worked in Russia as a freelance consultant. It was a similar role to the one I have now at Rowan Construction. The main difference is that I worked for myself. I had a company called Knowles Ltd. As a freelance consultant, I worked on many different building sites for many different companies. It was interesting, but I took the new post in London for better job security. My first job was at home in Ukraine. There, I was Graduate Engineer working for SKYBuild. This role involved using computer programmes to work on the design elements of buildings.

In terms of my qualifications, I've got a degree in Civil Engineering and a Masters in Structural Design. I'm also a member of the Institute of Civil Engineers, the UK's professional group for 'civils'.

I am an all-round employee; I work well in teams and on my own. For example, as Site Engineer for Rowan Construction, I have to manage each construction project. That involves working closely with the builders and architects. I have to be a good team player and communicator in order to do that successfully. On the other hand, in my Ukrainian job, I was the only person working on building designs, so I had to manage my own workload and didn't have a lot of communication with other company staff, apart from in meetings. That requires a lot of discipline.

Job4U Recruitment

Please answer each question truthfully.

Name: _____   Address: _____

Nationality: _____   Age: _____

Educational Qualifications

1. What third-level qualifications have you got? (Please tick.)

Certificate ☐	Field: _____
Diploma ☐	Field: _____
Degree ☐	Field: _____
Masters ☐	Field: _____
Doctorate ☐	Field: _____

2. What languages do you speak? (Please tick your level.)

Language: _____   Beginner ☐   Elementary ☐   Intermediate ☐
                 Upper-intermediate ☐   Advanced ☐   Full working proficiency ☐

Language: _____   Beginner ☐   Elementary ☐   Intermediate ☐
                 Upper-intermediate ☐   Advanced ☐   Full working proficiency ☐

Language: _____   Beginner ☐   Elementary ☐   Intermediate ☐
                 Upper-intermediate ☐   Advanced ☐   Full working proficiency ☐

Experience

1. Give details of your work experience (most recent first).

Job Title: _____   Company: _____

Role : _____

Job Title: _____   Company: _____

Role : _____

Job Title: _____   Company: _____

Role : _____

2. Please state any other relevant information, e.g. volunteer work, membership of professional groups.

_____
_____
_____
_____

Personal Qualities - Please outline your best personal qualities. Give examples.

_____
_____
_____
_____

Section 8

Have you got the right qualifications?

Exercise 1

A. Student 2 read Fran's career profile and use it to complete the Job4U Recruitment form that follows. Later, you will be Fran so get to know him/her well!

> Hi! I'm Fran. I come from Spain but have been living in the UK now for around 3 years – Flat 21, Beechcroft Place, Putney in London. I'm 28 years old and for the last three years, I've been a teacher of English at a school in Putney called Putney Grammar. My role involves helping teenagers who have recently moved to the UK to improve their English. Some speak very little when they arrive. Others are nearly fluent. Classes are mixed-level, so my job is very challenging. Before moving to the UK, I worked as a teaching assistant at a language school in Malta. I helped a very experienced teacher there and learned a lot from watching her classes. She taught young teens, both local and foreign students who came to Malta to learn English. My first role in teaching was as a volunteer teacher at a charity for poor immigrants in Spain. I taught people of all ages and levels of English there.
>
> I speak Spanish fluently – and, of course, English too. That's what I did my degree in. I then did a Masters in Education. I'm also a member of IATEFL, which is an English teachers' professional association.
>
> I've got a great relationship with my students – I think that's one of my real strengths. I'm very creative and can make the lessons fun and interesting. For example, last week we did a lesson on predicting the future. It's a grammar lesson, but I got the students to predict the future of famous celebrities and they really enjoyed it. Another thing I'm good at is lesson planning. I think carefully about each lesson before I teach it so that there is always a clear structure and a reason for learning. It helps the students follow and understand what I'm teaching them. I know what it's like to learn a foreign language so I want to make it easier, not harder for them. As well as learning English, I also did French at school. My French teacher used to make the lessons very complicated and I never did well in her class. Even today, I'm only intermediate level. Whereas, my English teacher was brilliant and I was fluent when I finished school.

Job4U Recruitment

Please answer each question truthfully.

Name: _____   Address: _____

Nationality: _____   Age: _____

Educational Qualifications

1. What third-level qualifications have you got? (Please tick.)

      Certificate ❑   Field: _____

      Diploma ❑   Field: _____

      Degree ❑   Field: _____

      Masters ❑   Field: _____

      Doctorate ❑   Field: _____

2. What languages do you speak? (Please tick your level.)

Language: _____   Beginner ❑   Elementary ❑   Intermediate ❑
                    Upper-intermediate ❑   Advanced ❑   Full working proficiency ❑

Language: _____   Beginner ❑   Elementary ❑   Intermediate ❑
                    Upper-intermediate ❑   Advanced ❑   Full working proficiency ❑

Language: _____   Beginner ❑   Elementary ❑   Intermediate ❑
                    Upper-intermediate ❑   Advanced ❑   Full working proficiency ❑

Experience

1. Give details of your work experience (most recent first).

    Job Title: _____   Company: _____

    Role : _____

    Job Title: _____   Company: _____

    Role : _____

    Job Title: _____   Company: _____

    Role : _____

2. Please state any other relevant information, e.g. volunteer work, membership of professional groups.

_____
_____
_____
_____

Personal Qualities - Please outline your best personal qualities. Give examples.

_____
_____
_____
_____

IELTS Life Skills

CEFR Level: B1

8

Exam preparation units

Unit 1

About the Listening section:
There are two parts to the Listening.

Part 1: You hear two recordings once. You have to listen and decide what each recording is about. You choose from the same three given options for each recording. The examiner will then ask you the answer for only one of the recordings. You don't know which one so you have to listen to both. You then say your answer. He/She will ask the other student about the second recording.

Part 2: You have to listen again to the recordings. This time you know which recording you must answer questions on before you listen. The examiner will ask you to listen to your recording for two specific pieces of information. You then say your answer when the recording has played.

Parts 1 and 2 involve different Listening skills.
Part 1 Listening skill: Listen for general idea or gist
Part 2 Listening skill: Listen for specific information

Part 1
You hear two people talking about themselves. What is each speaker mainly talking about? Their work life, their leisure activities or their relationships? 🎧

Note: When you do these practise exercises, always SAY your answers. If you are alone, speak into a mirror or similar. If you are in class, say your answers to a partner.

What is each speaker mainly talking about?

     their work life   **their leisure activities**   **their relationships**

Note: In the actual exam, you will be given a card like the one here, with the question and the options on it.

Part 2
Listen again and answer these questions. 🎧

∞ **In the first recording**, why did the speaker stop going to the cinema so often? And why did he stop hill walking?

∞ **In the second recording**, why did the speaker think it was important to make a career plan? And why did he choose mountain guiding as his second career?

Note: In this part, you are not given a card with the question on it like in Part 1. That means you have to listen carefully to the examiner. Listen to what the examiner says and make note of the two things to listen for if you want.

Note Taking: In the Listening, you CAN make notes. And it's always a good idea to take advantage of the opportunity to do so. Here, for example, if you make a note of the question, there is no chance of you forgetting it. Make a note of your answers while you listen for the same reason.

Speaking   Phase 1a

About Speaking Phase 1a:

There are a number of different Speaking tasks in the exam: Phase 1a, 1b, 2a and 2b.

Of course, you shouldn't think of these tasks as only 'speaking' because you also have to be an active listener in order to listen and respond to what the examiner and your partner say.

Here, in Phase 1a, you have to talk to the other student doing the exam with you for about two minutes. First, the examiner gives you a topic to discuss together. Then, you should speak and invite your partner to respond in order to have a discussion about the topic.

Don't worry if the examiner sometimes interrupts your conversation. He/She may want to ask you some questions that encourage the use of specific grammar.

Question: Now you are going to ask each other some questions. I want you to find out from each other about the sports and hobbies you used to do when you were younger and whether or not you like doing the same sports and hobbies today. You have two minutes to talk to each other.

Which sports or hobbies did you used to do?	I used to … How about you?
Do you still do the same sports and hobbies today?	Well, I still play … but I don't do …
Why don't you do … anymore?	Because I prefer … It's more relaxing/interesting/fun/etc.

How to practise speaking:

If you are in class, work with a partner. But what should you do if you are alone? Well, why not create an imaginary character? For example, in this question, make some notes about your imaginary character before you start. What sports and hobbies did they use to do? What sports and hobbies do they do today? Why are some of them different? Then, use a mirror or similar. You can do the speaking parts for both you and your imaginary character. Act it out just like a real conversation involving two different people.

Unit 2

Listening   Phase 2a

About the Listening section:
There are two parts to the Listening.

Part 1: You hear two recordings once. You have to listen and decide what each recording is about. You choose from the same three given options for each recording. The examiner will then ask you the answer for only one of the recordings. You don't know which one so you have to listen to both. You then say your answer. He/She will ask the other student about the second recording.

Part 2: You have to listen again to the recordings. This time you know which recording you must answer questions on before you listen. The examiner will ask you to listen to your recording for two specific pieces of information. You then say your answer when the recording has played.

Parts 1 and 2 involve different Listening skills.
Part 1 Listening skill: Listen for general idea or gist
Part 2 Listening skill: Listen for specific information

Part 1
You hear two weather forecasts. What is the weather for next week going to be like?
Mainly dry, mainly wet or mixed (some wet and some dry days)? 🎧

Note: When you do these practise exercises, always say your answers. If you are alone, speak into a mirror or similar. If you are in class, say your answers to a partner.

What is the weather for next week going to be like?

mainly dry   mainly wet   mixed
                                                          (some wet and some dry days)

Note: In the exam, you will be given a card like the one here with the question and the options on it.

Part 2
Listen again and answer these questions. 🎧

↪ **In the first recording**, what is the weather on Monday going to be like? And how are Thursday and Friday going to be different from Wednesday?

↪ **In the second recording**, why is Monday not going to be a very pleasant day? And what kind of a day is Wednesday going to be?

Note: In this part, you are not given a card with the question on it like in Part 1. That means you have to listen carefully to the examiner. Listen to what the examiner says and make note of the two things to listen for if you want.

Note Taking: In the Listening, you CAN make notes. And it's always a good idea to take advantage of the opportunity to do so. Here, for example, if you make a note of the question, there is no chance of you forgetting it. Make a note of your answers while you listen for the same reason.

Speaking　　　　　　　Phase 1b

About Speaking Phase 1b:

In Phase 1b, you talk on your own about a topic for around a minute and a half. Then, your partner asks you three questions about what you have said. Then you swap roles.

It's very important in this section to listen actively to your partner's speech. The examiner will know if you've been listening or not by the questions you ask your partner when they have finished talking.

Question: In this part of the test, you are each going to talk for about one and a half minutes. While you are talking, your partner will listen to you. Your partner will then ask you three questions about what you have said.

(*Candidate A*), you're going to tell (*Candidate B*) what the weather was like last week and how it affected you.

(*Candidate B*), you're going to tell (*Candidate A*) what the weather was like the last time you were on holiday and how it affected your holiday.

You both have one minute to think about what you want to say. You can make notes if you want to. If there's anything you don't understand, please ask.

Note Making: Use the minute you are given to make notes. Make your notes simple and easy to follow. Just write a few words that will help you remember each point you want to talk about. Use bullet points to make your notes clearer. For example:

Monday
- *rained all day*
- *football practice cancelled*

Tuesday
- *very windy*
- *trains delayed*
- *late for work*

Wednesday
- *sunny, fine day*
- *met friends for picnic in park after work*

Thursday & Friday
- *turned cold*
- *had to wear winter coat for 1st time this year*

Saturday & Sunday
- *snowed heavily*
- *football match cancelled*

(*Candidate A*), are you ready? Please tell (*Candidate B*) what the weather was like last week and how it affected you. (*Candidate B*), listen and ask three questions at the end.

(*Candidate B*), are you ready? Please tell (*Candidate A*) what the weather was like the last time you were on holiday and how it affected your holiday. (*Candidate A*), listen and ask three questions at the end.

Asking Questions: Practise forming questions in different tenses before the exam. Make sure you are comfortable doing this.

Unit 3

About the Listening section:
There are two parts to the Listening.

Part 1: You hear two recordings once. You have to listen and decide what each recording is about. You choose from the same three given options for each recording. The examiner will then ask you the answer for only one of the recordings. You don't know which one so you have to listen to both. You then say your answer. He/She will ask the other student about the second recording.

Part 2: You have to listen again to the recordings. This time you know which recording you must answer questions on before you listen. The examiner will ask you to listen to your recording for two specific pieces of information. You then say your answer when the recording has played.

Parts 1 and 2 involve different Listening skills.
Part 1 Listening skill: Listen for general idea or gist
Part 2 Listening skill: Listen for specific information

Part 1

You hear two people talking about their favourite holiday memories. Which type of holiday are they describing? A cruise holiday, an adventure holiday or a safari holiday? 🎧

Note: When you do these practise exercises, always say your answers. If you are alone, speak into a mirror or similar. If you are in class, say your answers to a partner.

Which type of holiday are they describing?

a cruise holiday   **an adventure holiday**   **a safari holiday**

Note: In the exam, you will be given a card like the one here with the question and the options on it.

Part 2

Listen again and answer these questions. 🎧

∞ **In the first recording**, why did the speaker and her husband travel by boat?
And what happened when the speaker saw the mountain lion?

∞ **In the second recording**, what reason does the speaker give for not getting sea sick?
And what was the speaker's most perfect memory of his trip to Antarctica?

Note: In this part, you are not given a card with the question on it like in Part 1. That means you have to listen carefully to the examiner. Listen to what the examiner says and make note of the two things to listen for if you want.

Note Taking: In the Listening, you CAN make notes. And it's always a good idea to take advantage of the opportunity to do so. Here, for example, if you make a note of the question, there is no chance of you forgetting it. Make a note of your answers while you listen for the same reason.

Speaking   Phase 1b

About Speaking Phase 1b:
In Phase 1b, you talk on your own about a topic for around a minute and a half. Then, your partner asks you three questions about what you have said. Then you swap roles.

It's very important in this section to listen actively to your partner's speech. The examiner will know if you've been listening or not by the questions you ask your partner when they have finished talking.

Question: In this part of the test, you are each going to talk for about one and a half minutes. While you are talking, your partner will listen to you. Your partner will then ask you three questions about what you have said.

(*Candidate A*), you're going to tell (*Candidate B*) what your most amazing holiday experience was and why you loved it so much.

(*Candidate B*), you're going to tell (*Candidate A*) what the most unusual thing you've ever done on holiday was and whether or not you enjoyed it.

You both have one minute to think about what you want to say. You can make notes if you want to. If there's anything you don't understand, please ask.

Note Making: Use the minute you are given to make notes. Make your notes simple and easy to follow. Just write a few words that will help you remember each point you want to talk about. Use bullet points to make your notes clearer.

(*Candidate A*), are you ready? Please tell (*Candidate B*) what your most amazing holiday experience was and why you loved it so much. (*Candidate B*), listen and ask three questions at the end.

(*Candidate B*), are you ready? Please tell (*Candidate A*) what the most unusual thing you've ever done on holiday was and whether or not you enjoyed it. (*Candidate A*), listen and ask three questions at the end.

Asking Questions: Let's have some practice on question forming.
Complete the questions with the correct question words or phrases.

1. **A:** _____ do you go on cruise holidays? **B:** I usually go once or twice a year.
2. **A:** _____ times have you been there? **B:** I've been there twice.
3. **A:** _____ do you usually do when you get there? **B:** We usually go sightseeing and take lots of photos.
4. **A:** _____ did you go with? **B:** I went with my husband and our two young children.
5. **A:** _____ should you visit? **B:** I would say April because the weather's lovely and there aren't too many tourists around.
6. **A:** _____ do you love it so much there? **B:** It's just a magical place. The scenery is amazing.

Unit 4

About the Listening section:
There are two parts to the Listening.

Part 1: You hear two recordings once. You have to listen and decide what each recording is about. You choose from the same three given options for each recording. The examiner will then ask you the answer for only one of the recordings. You don't know which one so you have to listen to both. You then say your answer. He/She will ask the other student about the second recording.

Part 2: You have to listen again to the recordings. This time you know which recording you must answer questions on before you listen. The examiner will ask you to listen to your recording for two specific pieces of information. You then say your answer when the recording has played.

Parts 1 and 2 involve different Listening skills.
Part 1 Listening skill: Listen for general idea or gist
Part 2 Listening skill: Listen for specific information

Part 1
You hear two people talking about their health problems. What problem are they describing?
A headache, an allergy or a broken arm? 🎧

Note: When you do these practise exercises, always say your answers. If you are alone, speak into a mirror or similar. If you are in class, say your answers to a partner.

What problem are they describing?

        a headache   an allergy   a broken arm

Note: In the exam, you will be given a card like the one here with the question and the options on it.

Part 2
Listen again and answer these questions. 🎧

- **In the first recording**, why did the speaker's wife get scared and call an ambulance? And how long did it take the speaker to get better?

- **In the second recording**, what did the speaker wear on his legs? And what was the actual temperature that day at the ski resort?

Note: In this part, you are not given a card with the question on it like in Part 1. That means you have to listen carefully to the examiner. Listen to what the examiner says and make note of the two things to listen for if you want.

Note Taking: In the Listening, you CAN make notes. And it's always a good idea to take advantage of the opportunity to do so. Here, for example, if you make a note of the question, there is no chance of you forgetting it. Make a note of your answers while you listen for the same reason.

Speaking   Phase 1b

About Speaking Phase 1b:

In Phase 1b, you talk on your own about a topic for around a minute and a half. Then, your partner asks you three questions about what you have said. Then you swap roles.

It's very important in this section to listen actively to your partner's speech. The examiner will know if you've been listening or not by the questions you ask your partner when they have finished talking.

Question: In this part of the test, you are each going to talk for about one and a half minutes. While you are talking, your partner will listen to you. Your partner will then ask you three questions about what you have said.

(Candidate A), you're going to tell (Candidate B) about a time when you were ill and what you did about it.

(Candidate B), you're going to tell (Candidate A) about the last time you missed work, college or an event because of sickness and what was wrong with you.

You both have one minute to think about what you want to say. You can make notes if you want to. If there's anything you don't understand, please ask.

Note Making: Use the minute you are given to make notes. Make your notes simple and easy to follow. Just write a few words that will help you remember each point you want to talk about. Use bullet points to make your notes clearer.

(Candidate A), are you ready? Please tell (Candidate B) about a time when you were ill and what you did about it. (Candidate B), listen and ask three questions at the end.

(Candidate B), are you ready? Please tell (Candidate A) about the last time you missed work, college or an event because of sickness and what was wrong with you. (Candidate A), listen and ask three questions at the end.

Asking Questions: Let's have some practice on question forming.
Complete each question with the correct form of the verb in brackets.

1. What _____ you _____ when you found out your temperature was 39 degrees? **(do)**
2. _____ it _____ you long to recover? **(take)**
3. _____ you able to get some sleep? **(be)**
4. _____ you ever _____ a serious illness? **(have)**
5. _____ you ever _____ so sick that you had to go to hospital? **(be)**
6. How _____ you _____ now – have you fully recovered? **(feel)**

Unit 5

Part 1

You hear two people talking about food. What type of meal did they have? A home-cooked meal, a restaurant meal or a takeaway meal? 🎧

What type of meal did they have?

    a home-cooked meal   **a restaurant meal**   **a takeaway meal**

Part 2

Listen again and answer these questions. 🎧

∞ **In the first recording**, why did they choose a place beside the sea? And what main course did the speaker have?

∞ **In the second recording**, where had the speaker and her family been all day? And what did the speaker dislike about the place they got food from?

About Speaking Phase 2b, Part 1:

In this section, you and your partner must work together to plan something. The examiner will give you a card with things to discuss and you should talk together for about two minutes and come to an agreement on what to do.

Don't worry if the examiner interrupts you to ask questions. This is normal.

Question: Now you're going to plan something together. I'd like you to imagine that you are going to have a dinner party. First, talk together about what you should do about preparing the food and choose the best option. Then, plan and decide what to do about these things. You have two minutes to talk about this, so don't worry if I interrupt you. Would you like to start now?

Prompt Card: In this part of the exam, you are always given a prompt card with points to discuss, just like the one below. Make sure you discuss all the points on the prompt card. The first question on the prompt card involves you making a choice between three different things. Make sure you come to an agreement with your partner on one of them. The second question involves deciding the details of what to do.

What to do about preparing the food?	Plan and decide
• get takeaway • cook ourselves • hire a chef	• how many courses to have • what dishes should be on the menu • what drinks to serve

The first question

Briefly give and explain your opinion on all three options, which one you prefer and why.
Make sure you allow your partner the chance to do this as well.
Then, come to a decision; agree on one option.

Give your opinion

I think ... is a good idea because ...
I don't like the idea of ... because ...

Invite your partner's opinion

What do you think?
Do you agree?

Suggest a decision

OK. Let's ... , shall we?
OK. So shall we ... ?

The second question

Make suggestions for each point. Invite your partner to agree or share their ideas.
Then come to a decision on what to do.

Make suggestions

Why don't we ... ?
How about ... ?

Ask for your partner's ideas

What do you think?
Have you got any ideas?

Come to a decision and sum up

OK, so we're going to ...
Is that right?
Let's ... , shall we?

Speaking   Phase 2b

About Speaking Phase 2b, Part 2:
There is then a second part of Phase 2b, where you have to discuss a related topic with your partner for about 3-4 minutes.

The examiner may interrupt your discussion to ask questions and/or develop the topic.

Question: Now you're going to talk together about healthy eating. Talk to each other about the kinds of food you eat every day and how you could improve your diet and make it healthier.

Keep the conversation going

In order to keep your discussion going, you should practise the following conversation skills:

Giving your opinion and inviting a response
I think ... And you?
My belief is that ... What do you think?
In my view ... Would you agree?

Agreeing and disagreeing politely
Agreeing:
I totally agree with you.
I know what you mean.
That's a good point.

Disagreeing politely:
I see what you are saying, but ...
I know what you mean, but ...
I take your point, but ...

Changing what you are talking about / introducing a new idea
What about ... [new idea] ?
Let's talk about ... [new idea].
Another thing to talk/think about is ... [new idea].

Unit 6

About the Listening section:
There are two parts to the Listening.

Part 1: You hear two recordings once. You have to listen and decide what each recording is about. You choose from the same three given options for each recording. The examiner will then ask you the answer for only one of the recordings. You don't know which one so you have to listen to both. You then say your answer. He/She will ask the other student about the second recording.

Part 2: You have to listen again to the recordings. This time you know which recording you must answer questions on before you listen. The examiner will ask you to listen to your recording for two specific pieces of information. You then say your answer when the recording has played.

Parts 1 and 2 involve different Listening skills.
Part 1 Listening skill: Listen for general idea or gist
Part 2 Listening skill: Listen for specific information

Part 1
You hear two people talking about how they get to work. What type of transport do they use?
A car, the train or a taxi? 🎧

Note: When you do these practise exercises, always say your answers. If you are alone, speak into a mirror or similar. If you are in class, say your answers to a partner.

What type of transport do they use?

a car	the train	a taxi

Note: In the exam, you will be given a card like the one here with the question and the options on it.

Part 2
Listen again and answer these questions. 🎧

↪ **In the first recording**, why does the speaker get annoyed? And why does the speaker dislike travelling by train?

↪ **In the second recording**, why does the speaker get free travel? And what method of transport will the speaker use after her three months of free travel are up?

Note: In this part, you are not given a card with the question on it like in Part 1. That means you have to listen carefully to the examiner. Listen to what the examiner says and make note of the two things to listen for if you want.

Note Taking: In the Listening, you CAN make notes. And it's always a good idea to take advantage of the opportunity to do so. Here, for example, if you make a note of the question, there is no chance of you forgetting it. Make a note of your answers while you listen for the same reason.

Speaking   Phase 2b

About Speaking Phase 2b, Part 1:
In this section, you and your partner must work together to plan something. The examiner will give you a card with things to discuss and you should talk together for about two minutes and come to an agreement on what to do.

Don't worry if the examiner interrupts you to ask questions. This is normal.

Question: Now you're going to plan something together. I'd like you to imagine that you are going to go on a trip around the UK. First, talk together about what way you should travel and choose the best option. Then, plan and decide what to do about these things. You have two minutes to talk about this, so don't worry if I interrupt you. Would you like to start now?

Prompt Card: In this part of the exam, you are always given a prompt card with points to discuss, just like the one below. Make sure you discuss all the points on the prompt card. The first question on the prompt card involves you making a choice between three different things. Make sure you come to an agreement with your partner on one of them. The second question involves deciding the details of what to do.

How to travel around the UK?	Plan and decide
• hitchhike • use public transport • rent a car	• when to go • what to pack • where to stay – hotels, hostels, etc.

Useful phrases

1. Giving and explaining an opinion.	2. Inviting a reply.	
	a. asking for agreement	b. asking for an opinion
To my mind, the best option is to … because …	Wouldn't you agree?	What do you think?
I feel that we should … because …	Don't you think?	What's your view?
I'm not keen on … because …	Wouldn't you say?	How do you see it?

Question: Now you're going to talk together about transport. Talk to each other about the different forms of transport you use, which forms you like, which forms you dislike and why.

Unit 7

Listening   Phase 2a

About the Listening section:
There are two parts to the Listening.

Part 1: You hear two recordings once. You have to listen and decide what each recording is about. You choose from the same three given options for each recording. The examiner will then ask you the answer for only one of the recordings. You don't know which one so you have to listen to both. You then say your answer. He/She will ask the other student about the second recording.

Part 2: You have to listen again to the recordings. This time you know which recording you must answer questions on before you listen. The examiner will ask you to listen to your recording for two specific pieces of information. You then say your answer when the recording has played.

Parts 1 and 2 involve different Listening skills.
Part 1 Listening skill: Listen for general idea or gist
Part 2 Listening skill: Listen for specific information

Part 1
You hear two people talking about a family member. Who are they talking about?
A cousin, an aunt or a sibling? 🎧

Note: When you do these practise exercises, always say your answers. If you are alone, speak into a mirror or similar. If you are in class, say your answers to a partner.

Who are they talking about?

　　　　a cousin　　　　　　　　an aunt　　　　　　　　a sibling

Note: In the exam, you will be given a card like the one here with the question and the options on it.

Part 2
Listen again and answer these questions. 🎧

∽ **In the first recording,** who is older – Marie or the speaker? And how old was Marie when she first started to hang out with the speaker?

∽ **In the second recording,** how did Aunt May and Uncle Tommy treat the speaker differently to James? And, growing up, why was James happy to have the speaker around?

Note: In this part, you are not given a card with the question on it like in Part 1. That means you have to listen carefully to the examiner. Listen to what the examiner says and make note of the two things to listen for if you want.

Note Taking: In the Listening, you CAN make notes. And it's always a good idea to take advantage of the opportunity to do so. Here, for example, if you make a note of the question, there is no chance of you forgetting it. Make a note of your answers while you listen for the same reason.

Speaking   Phase 2b

About Speaking Phase 2b, Part 1:
In this section, you and your partner must work together to plan something. The examiner will give you a card with things to discuss and you should talk together for about two minutes and come to an agreement on what to do.

Don't worry if the examiner interrupts you to ask questions. This is normal.

Question: Now you're going to plan something together. I'd like you to imagine that you are booking a holiday home. First, talk together about what type of home you should rent and choose the best option. Then, plan and decide what features your holiday home needs to have. You have two minutes to talk about this, so don't worry if I interrupt you. Would you like to start now?

Prompt Card: In this part of the exam, you are always given a prompt card with points to discuss, just like the one below. Make sure you discuss all the points on the prompt card. The first question on the prompt card involves you making a choice between three different things. Make sure you come to an agreement with your partner on one of them. The second question involves deciding the details of what to do.

What type of holiday home should it be?	Plan and decide – holiday home features
• flat • cottage • large house	• location – city or countryside • what facilities – parking, internet, etc. • what appliances – washing machine, TV, etc.

Useful phrases

We should probably book a house in …

It's important to have …

We'll definitely need …

Question: Now you're going to talk together about housing. Talk to each other about the living conditions where you come from – what kinds of homes most people have, how expensive housing is and whether or not there is a homelessness problem.

Unit 8

About the Listening section:
There are two parts to the Listening.

Part 1: You hear two recordings once. You have to listen and decide what each recording is about. You choose from the same three given options for each recording. The examiner will then ask you the answer for only one of the recordings. You don't know which one so you have to listen to both. You then say your answer. He/She will ask the other student about the second recording.

Part 2: You have to listen again to the recordings. This time you know which recording you must answer questions on before you listen. The examiner will ask you to listen to your recording for two specific pieces of information. You then say your answer when the recording has played.

Parts 1 and 2 involve different Listening skills.
Part 1 Listening skill: Listen for general idea or gist
Part 2 Listening skill: Listen for specific information

Part 1

You hear two people talking about their education. What part of their education are they talking about? Primary school, secondary school or university? 🎧

Note: When you do these practise exercises, always say your answers. If you are alone, speak into a mirror or similar. If you are in class, say your answers to a partner.

What part of their education are they talking about?

primary school   secondary school   university

Note: In the exam, you will be given a card like the one here with the question and the options on it.

Part 2

Listen again and answer these questions. 🎧

☞ **In the first recording**, why was the speaker not nervous on the first day of school? And what examples does the speaker give of technology that her school didn't have?

☞ **In the second recording**, when did the speaker's opinion of school change for the better? And how did the speaker feel about her long school study sessions at the time?

Note: In this part, you are not given a card with the question on it like in Part 1. That means you have to listen carefully to the examiner. Listen to what the examiner says and make note of the two things to listen for if you want.

Note Taking: In the Listening, you CAN make notes. And it's always a good idea to take advantage of the opportunity to do so. Here, for example, if you make a note of the question, there is no chance of you forgetting it. Make a note of your answers while you listen for the same reason.

Speaking   Phase 1a

About Speaking Phase 1a:

There are a number of different Speaking tasks in the exam: Phase 1a, 1b, 2a and 2b.

Of course, you shouldn't think of these tasks as only 'speaking' because you also have to be an active listener in order to listen and respond to what the examiner and your partner say.

Here, in Phase 1a, you have to talk to the other student doing the exam with you for about two minutes. First, the examiner gives you a topic to discuss together. Then, you should speak and invite your partner to respond in order to have a discussion about the topic.

Don't worry if the examiner sometimes interrupts your conversation. He/She may want to ask you some questions that encourage the use of specific grammar.

Question: Now you are going to ask each other some questions. I want you to find out from each other about your educational and work backgrounds. You have two minutes to talk to each other.

> What do you do for a living?

> I work as a …
> I'm a housewife / house husband / student.

> Did you go to university?

> Yes, I studied … at …
> No. I started a family.
> I'm between jobs.

> Do you have happy memories of your school years?

> Well, yes. Especially … because …
> To be honest, I didn't really like … because …

How to practise speaking:

If you are in class, work with a partner. But what should you do if you are alone? Well, why not create an imaginary character? For example, in this question, make some notes about your imaginary character before you start. What sports and hobbies did they use to do? What sports and hobbies do they do today? Why are some of them different? Then, use a mirror or similar. You can do the speaking parts for both you and your imaginary character. Act it out just like a real conversation involving two different people.

IELTS Life Skills

CEFR Level B1

6

Practice Tests

Test 1

B1 Speaking and Listening

This test should not exceed 22 minutes.

Please note: With the exception of the Task Sheets in Phases 2a and 2b, this sample test frame will be used only by the Examiner. It will not be shown to the candidates.

3 minutes   Phase 1a

Hello. My name is _____ (Examiner).

[Ask Candidate A and Candidate B in turn questions about name and nationality (see below).]

Name	What's your name? Can you spell it for me?
Nationality	Where do you come from? How long have you lived here?

Thank you. Could I have your marksheets? *[Collect marksheets.]*

Thank you.

Now you are going to ask each other some questions. I want you to find out from each other about your hometown and why you like or dislike it. You have two minutes to talk to each other.

[Withdraw eye contact to signal that candidates should start. Allow two minutes. Prompt candidates with questions from the box below, or others suitable for the level, if necessary (e.g. if interaction breaks down or if language remains below B1 level).]

> **Prompt questions:**
>
> What can you do there?
>
> How is _____ different from / similar to _____ ?
>
> What is the best/worst thing about _____?
>
> What would you like to change about your hometown?

Thank you.

7 minutes   **Phase 1b**

In this part of the test, you are each going to talk for about one and a half minutes. While you are talking, your partner will listen to you. Your partner will then ask you three questions about what you have said.

_____ (Candidate A), **you're going to tell** _____ (Candidate B) **about an activity you'd like to try and why you'd like to try it.**

_____ (Candidate B), **you're going to tell** _____ (Candidate A) **about a friend you really trust and why you trust them so much.**

You both have one minute to think about what you want to say. You can make notes if you want to. [Indicate paper and pencil.] **If there's anything you don't understand, please ask me.**

[Withdraw eye contact to signal start of preparation. Allow 1 minute for preparation.]

_____ (Candidate A), **are you ready? Please tell** _____ (Candidate B) **about an activity you'd like to try and why you'd like to try it.** _____ (Candidate B), **listen, and ask three questions at the end.** [Allow 1½ minutes.]

Thank you. _____ (Candidate B), **please ask** _____ (Candidate A) **your questions now.**

Thank you.

_____ (Candidate B), **are you ready? Please tell** _____ (Candidate A) **about a friend you really trust and why you trust them so much.** _____ (Candidate A), **listen, and ask three questions at the end.** [Allow 1½ minutes.]

Thank you. _____ (Candidate A), **please ask** _____ (Candidate B) **your questions now.**

Thank you.

5 minutes   Phase 2a

In this part of the test, you are going to listen to two recordings and answer some questions. You can make notes *[indicate paper]* if you want to.

You hear two messages about different types of transport. *[Hand each candidate the booklet open at the correct page.]* What type of transport is each message about? A plane, a car or a ferry?

What type of transport is each message about?

        a plane   a car   a ferry

Listen to the information. *[Play CD.]*

_____ (Candidate A), in the first recording, what type of transport is the message about? A plane, a car or a ferry?

Thank you.

_____ (Candidate B), in the second recording, what type of transport is the message about? A plane, a car or a ferry?

Thank you. *[Retrieve booklets.]*

Now listen again, and answer these questions.

_____ (Candidate B), in the first recording, what is the new departure time of the ship? *[short pause]* And what can each passenger get for free?

_____ (Candidate A), in the second recording, what time should Nora get to the Information Desk by? *[short pause]* And what will happen to her vehicle if she's late?

*[Play CD again: scripts as above. At the end of the recording ask each candidate in turn their two questions again. After **each** question, **wait** for the candidate's response.]*

Thank you.

7 minutes overall   Phase 2b

✳ **3 minutes**

Now you're going to plan something together.

I'd like you to imagine that a friend is planning a weekend away in the countryside with her elderly parents. She wants your advice on what to do. [Hand out candidate booklet at correct page.]

First talk together about which transport she should use for the weekend away and choose the one you think would be best. [Read out list while pointing at the first box.]

Then plan and decide what to do about these things. [Read out list while pointing at the second box.]

You have two minutes to talk about this, so don't worry if I interrupt you.

[Withdraw eye contact to signal that candidates should start. If candidates do not start within 10 seconds, ask: **Would you like to start now?**]

Which transport?	Plan and decide
• car • train • bus	• what to pack • the best type of accommodation • the best activities

Thank you.
[Retrieve candidate booklets.]

✳ **4 minutes**

Now you're going to talk together about transport. Talk to each other about the transport facilities where you live and whether they are good or bad.

[Repeat if necessary. Withdraw eye contact to signal start of activity.

If necessary, prompt candidates with questions from the box below (e.g. if students are experiencing difficulty in continuing the interaction or if they stray from the topic). Adapt if necessary. Encourage candidate-candidate interaction by eliciting agreement or alternative opinions from candidates by asking questions such as "What do you think?", "Tell us what you think.", "And you?"]

> Transport facilities where you live – prompt questions
>
> Do the buses/trains ever arrive late?
> How often do the buses/trains stop every hour?
> Is your area a safe place to cycle? Why? / Why not?
> What do you think are the advantages and disadvantages of travelling by bus/train/car?

Thank you. That is the end of the test.
[Ensure candidates DO NOT leave the room with the candidate booklet.]

Test 2

B1 Speaking and Listening

This test should not exceed 22 minutes.

> *Please note:* With the exception of the Task Sheets in Phases 2a and 2b, this sample test frame will be used only by the Examiner. It will not be shown to the candidates.

3 minutes   Phase 1a

Hello. My name is _____ (Examiner).
[Ask Candidate A and Candidate B in turn questions about name and nationality (see below).]

Name	What's your name? Can you spell it for me?
Nationality	Where do you come from? How long have you lived here?

Thank you. Could I have your marksheets? *[Collect marksheets.]*

Thank you.

Now you are going to ask each other some questions. I want you to find out from each other about your living situation – where you live and what's good or bad about it. You have two minutes to talk to each other.

[Withdraw eye contact to signal that candidates should start. Allow two minutes. Prompt candidates with questions from the box below, or others suitable for the level, if necessary (e.g. if interaction breaks down or if language remains below B1 level).]

> **Prompt questions:**
>
> What kind of building is it?
>
> What is your neighbourhood like?
>
> How long have you lived there?
>
> What would you like to change about your living situation?

Thank you.

7 minutes   **Phase 1b**

In this part of the test, you are each going to talk for about one and a half minutes. While you are talking, your partner will listen to you. Your partner will then ask you three questions about what you have said.

_____ (Candidate A), **you're going to tell** _____ (Candidate B) **about an unusual building or place you visited and why it was unusual.**

_____ (Candidate B), **you're going to tell** _____ (Candidate A) **about a time you had to go to the doctor or the hospital, what was wrong and how you felt.**

You both have one minute to think about what you want to say. You can make notes if you want to. [Indicate paper and pencil.] **If there's anything you don't understand, please ask me.**

[Withdraw eye contact to signal start of preparation. Allow 1 minute for preparation.]

_____ (Candidate A), **are you ready? Please tell** _____ (Candidate B) **about an unusual building or place you visited and why it was unusual.** _____ (Candidate B), **listen, and ask three questions at the end.** [Allow 1½ minutes.]

Thank you. _____ (Candidate B), **please ask** _____ (Candidate A) **your questions now.**

Thank you.

_____ (Candidate B), **are you ready? Please tell** _____ (Candidate A) **about a time you had to go to the doctor or the hospital, what was wrong and how you felt.** _____ (Candidate A), **listen, and ask three questions at the end.** [Allow 1½ minutes.]

Thank you. _____ (Candidate A), **please ask** _____ (Candidate B) **your questions now.**

Thank you.

Test 2

In this part of the test, you are going to listen to two recordings and answer some questions. You can make notes [indicate paper] if you want to.

You hear two answerphone messages about holidays. [Hand each candidate the booklet open at the correct page.] What holiday type is each message about? A weekend city break, a sun/beach holiday or an adventure holiday?

What holiday type is each message about?

     a weekend city break   a sun/beach holiday   an adventure holiday

---

Listen to the information. [Play CD.]

_____ (Candidate A), **in the first recording, what type of holiday is the message about? A weekend city break, a sun/beach holiday or an adventure holiday?**

Thank you.

_____ (Candidate B), **in the second recording, what type of holiday is the message about? A weekend city break, a sun/beach holiday or an adventure holiday?**

Thank you. [Retrieve booklets.]

Now listen again, and answer these questions.

_____ (Candidate B), **in the first recording, why can't Jeff go on the trip?** [short pause] **And what day does Dawn fly to her holiday destination?**

_____ (Candidate A), **in the second recording, what's the weather forecast for Monday?** [short pause] **And why does Rod want to do the surfing lessons at the weekend?**

[Play CD again: scripts as above. At the end of the recording ask each candidate in turn their two questions again. After **each** question, **wait** for the candidate's response.]

Thank you.

7 minutes overall   Phase 2b

✻ **3 minutes**

Now you're going to plan something together.

I'd like you to imagine that you are two friends planning an active holiday. *[Hand out candidate booklet at correct page.]*

First talk together about which type of holiday you should go on and choose the one you think would be best. *[Read out list while pointing at the first box.]*

Then plan and decide what to do about these things. *[Read out list while pointing at the second box.]*

You have two minutes to talk about this, so don't worry if I interrupt you.

[Withdraw eye contact to signal that candidates should start. If candidates do not start within 10 seconds, ask: **Would you like to start now?***]*

Which holiday?	Plan and decide
• winter sports • water sports • tennis camp	• what time of year to go • what to pack • whether to rent or buy equipment

Thank you.
[Retrieve candidate booklets.]

✻ **4 minutes**

Now you're going to talk together about travel and holidays. Talk to each other about the advantages and disadvantages of holidaying abroad and holidaying in your home country.

[Repeat if necessary. Withdraw eye contact to signal start of activity.

If necessary, prompt candidates with questions from the box below (e.g. if students are experiencing difficulty in continuing the interaction or if they stray from the topic). Adapt if necessary. Encourage candidate-candidate interaction by eliciting agreement or alternative opinions from candidates by asking questions such as "What do you think?", "Tell us what you think.", "And you?"]

> **Holidaying abroad or in your home country – prompt questions**
>
> What can go wrong when you are on holiday in a foreign country?
> Do you think people miss out on some experiences if they never go on holiday abroad?
> Think about the places tourists visit in your country; have you ever visited those places? Why? / Why not?
> Which is harder to organise - a holiday at home or abroad? Which is more expensive?

Thank you. That is the end of the test.
[Ensure candidates DO NOT leave the room with the candidate booklet.]

Test 3

B1 Speaking and Listening

This test should not exceed 22 minutes.

Please note: With the exception of the Task Sheets in Phases 2a and 2b, this sample test frame will be used only by the Examiner. It will not be shown to the candidates.

3 minutes — Phase 1a

Hello. My name is _____ (Examiner).
[Ask Candidate A and Candidate B in turn questions about name and nationality (see below).]

Name	What's your name? Can you spell it for me?
Nationality	Where do you come from? How long have you lived here?

Thank you. Could I have your marksheets? *[Collect marksheets.]*

Thank you.

Now you are going to ask each other some questions. I want you to find out from each other about what you do for a living now and what job you would like to do in the future. You have two minutes to talk to each other.

[Withdraw eye contact to signal that candidates should start. Allow two minutes. Prompt candidates with questions from the box below, or others suitable for the level, if necessary (e.g. if interaction breaks down or if language remains below B1 level).]

> Prompt questions:
>
> Do you have a job at the moment? (Do you enjoy it? Why? / Why not?)
> (If not: What do you do instead?)
>
> Which do you think is more important – the amount of money you earn or how much you enjoy your job?
>
> Would you prefer an office job or a job working outdoors? Why?
>
> What would be your perfect job?

Thank you.

7 minutes   **Phase 1b**

In this part of the test, you are each going to talk for about one and a half minutes. While you are talking, your partner will listen to you. Your partner will then ask you three questions about what you have said.

_____ (Candidate A), **you're going to tell** _____ (Candidate B) **about your memories of your early school days and whether you enjoyed school or not.**

_____ (Candidate B), **you're going to tell** _____ (Candidate A) **about your first job and whether it was a good or bad experience.**

You both have one minute to think about what you want to say. You can make notes if you want to. *[Indicate paper and pencil.]* **If there's anything you don't understand, please ask me.**

[Withdraw eye contact to signal start of preparation. Allow 1 minute for preparation.]

_____ (Candidate A), **are you ready? Please tell** _____ (Candidate B) **about your memories of your early school days and whether you enjoyed school or not.** _____ (Candidate B), **listen, and ask three questions at the end.** *[Allow 1½ minutes.]*

Thank you. _____ (Candidate B), **please ask** _____ (Candidate A) **your questions now.**

Thank you.

_____ (Candidate B), **are you ready? Please tell** _____ (Candidate A) **about your first job and whether it was a good or bad experience.** _____ (Candidate A), **listen, and ask three questions at the end.** *[Allow 1½ minutes.]*

Thank you. _____ (Candidate A), **please ask** _____ (Candidate B) **your questions now.**

Thank you.

Test 3

5 minutes   Phase 2a

In this part of the test, you are going to listen to two recordings and answer some questions. You can make notes *[indicate paper]* if you want to.

You hear two messages about work. *[Hand each candidate the booklet open at the correct page.]*
What is the speaker's job? A journalist, a nurse or a prison officer?

What is the speaker's job?

        a journalist   **a nurse**   **a prison officer**

Listen to the information. *[Play CD.]*

_____ *(Candidate A)*, **in the first recording, what is the speaker's job? A journalist, a nurse or a prison officer?**

Thank you.

_____ *(Candidate B)*, **in the second recording, what is the speaker's job? A journalist, a nurse or a prison officer?**

Thank you. *[Retrieve booklets.]*

Now listen again, and answer these questions.

_____ *(Candidate B)*, **in the first recording, why will Fi be late home from work?** *[short pause]* **And what is she going to do about the problem she talks about?**

_____ *(Candidate A)*, **in the second recording, what did Phil just finish and send to his workplace?** *[short pause]* **And what does he want to talk to the newspaper about when he gets back?**

*[Play CD again: scripts as above. At the end of the recording ask each candidate in turn their two questions again. After **each** question, **wait** for the candidate's response.]*

Thank you.

7 minutes overall   Phase 2b

✳ **3 minutes**

Now you're going to plan something together.

I'd like you to imagine that you work for the post office and are hiring a new postman or woman. *[Hand out candidate booklet at correct page.]*

First talk together about where you should advertise the job and choose the place you think would be best. *[Read out list while pointing at the first box.]*

Then consider and decide what to do about these things. *[Read out list while pointing at the second box.]*

You have two minutes to talk about this, so don't worry if I interrupt you.

[Withdraw eye contact to signal that candidates should start. If candidates do not start within 10 seconds, ask: **Would you like to start now?***]*

Where to advertise the job	Consider and decide
• local newspaper • post office noticeboard • internet job site	• what skills the job requires • what type of person you want to hire • what their salary should be

Thank you.
[Retrieve candidate booklets.]

✳ **4 minutes**

Now you're going to talk together about work. Talk to each other about the things that make people happy in their job, and say which ones are the most important.

[Repeat if necessary. Withdraw eye contact to signal start of activity.

If necessary, prompt candidates with questions from the box below (e.g. if students are experiencing difficulty in continuing the interaction or if they stray from the topic). Adapt if necessary. Encourage candidate-candidate interaction by eliciting agreement or alternative opinions from candidates by asking questions such as "What do you think?", "Tell us what you think.", "And you?"]

> **Things that make people happy in their job – prompt questions**
>
> Are the people you work with important? What should you do if you don't like your manager?
> Would you be happy in a very stressful job if you also had a very high salary?
> What other things apart from pay are important to look for in a job? Is pay the most important thing?
> In what ways can working long hours become a serious problem?

Thank you. That is the end of the test.
[Ensure candidates DO NOT leave the room with the candidate booklet.]

Test 4

B1 Speaking and Listening

This test should not exceed 22 minutes.

> *Please note:* With the exception of the Task Sheets in Phases 2a and 2b, this sample test frame will be used only by the Examiner. It will not be shown to the candidates.

3 minutes   Phase 1a

Hello. My name is _____ (Examiner).

[Ask Candidate A and Candidate B in turn questions about name and nationality (see below).]

Name	What's your name? Can you spell it for me?
Nationality	Where do you come from? How long have you lived here?

Thank you. Could I have your marksheets? *[Collect marksheets.]*

Thank you.

Now you are going to ask each other some questions. I want you to find out from each other about your favourite and least favourite kinds of weather, and why you like or dislike them. You have two minutes to talk to each other.

[Withdraw eye contact to signal that candidates should start. Allow two minutes. Prompt candidates with questions from the box below, or others suitable for the level, if necessary (e.g. if interaction breaks down or if language remains below B1 level).]

> **Prompt questions:**
>
> Do you prefer when it's warm or cool? Why?
>
> It often rains in Britain. Does this make you want to live somewhere else?
>
> Which is worse – hot, wet weather or cold, dry weather? Why?
>
> What would be the climate of your perfect place to live?

Thank you.

7 minutes   Phase 1b

In this part of the test, you are each going to talk for about one and a half minutes. While you are talking, your partner will listen to you. Your partner will then ask you three questions about what you have said.

_____ (Candidate A), **you're going to tell** _____ (Candidate B) **about a really good gift you received and what made it so special.**

_____ (Candidate B), **you're going to tell** _____ (Candidate A) **about a time when the weather forced you to change your plans and what happened as a result.**

You both have one minute to think about what you want to say. You can make notes if you want to. [Indicate paper and pencil.] **If there's anything you don't understand, please ask me.**

[Withdraw eye contact to signal start of preparation. Allow 1 minute for preparation.]

_____ (Candidate A), **are you ready? Please tell** _____ (Candidate B) **about a really good gift you received and what made it so special.** _____ (Candidate B), **listen, and ask three questions at the end.** [Allow 1½ minutes.]

Thank you. _____ (Candidate B), **please ask** _____ (Candidate A) **your questions now.**

Thank you.

_____ (Candidate B), **are you ready? Please tell** _____ (Candidate A) **about a time when the weather forced you to change your plans and what happened as a result.** _____ (Candidate A), **listen, and ask three questions at the end.** [Allow 1½ minutes.]

Thank you. _____ (Candidate A), **please ask** _____ (Candidate B) **your questions now.**

Thank you.

5 minutes   **Phase 2a**

In this part of the test, you are going to listen to two recordings and answer some questions. You can make notes *[indicate paper]* **if you want to.**

You hear two messages left on answerphones. *[Hand each candidate the booklet open at the correct page.]* **What is the relationship of the speaker to the person the message is for? Husband, son or father?**

What is the relationship of the speaker to the person the message is for?

     husband   **son**   **father**

Listen to the information. *[Play CD.]*

_____ *(Candidate A),* **in the first recording, what is the relationship of the speaker to the person the message is for? Husband, son or father?**

Thank you.

_____ *(Candidate B),* **in the second recording, what is the relationship of the speaker to the person the message is for? Husband, son or father?**

Thank you. *[Retrieve booklets.]*

Now listen again, and answer these questions.

_____ *(Candidate B),* **in the first recording, why is the speaker late?** *[short pause]* **And where will Rach wait to get collected today?**

_____ *(Candidate A),* **in the second recording, for how long was the person in Spain?** *[short pause]* **And why does the speaker think his dad was lonely or unhappy?**

*[Play CD again: scripts as above. At the end of the recording ask each candidate in turn their two questions again. After **each** question, **wait** for the candidate's response.]*

Thank you.

7 minutes overall   **Phase 2b**

✳ 3 minutes

Now you're going to plan something together.

I'd like you to imagine that you are planning a birthday party for your best friend. *[Hand out candidate booklet at correct page.]*

First talk together about where the party should be held and choose the place you think would be best. *[Read out list while pointing at the first box.]*

Then plan and decide what to do about these things. *[Read out list while pointing at the second box.]*

You have two minutes to talk about this, so don't worry if I interrupt you.

[Withdraw eye contact to signal that candidates should start. If candidates do not start within 10 seconds, ask: **Would you like to start now?***]*

Which place?	Plan and decide
• a restaurant • a theme park • one of your homes	• when to have the party and how many people to invite • what food and drinks to have • what present to get

Thank you.
[Retrieve candidate booklets.]

✳ 4 minutes

Now you're going to talk together about friendship. Talk to each other about the qualities you value in a good friend.

[Repeat if necessary. Withdraw eye contact to signal start of activity.

If necessary, prompt candidates with questions from the box below (e.g. if students are experiencing difficulty in continuing the interaction or if they stray from the topic). Adapt if necessary. Encourage candidate-candidate interaction by eliciting agreement or alternative opinions from candidates by asking questions such as "What do you think?", "Tell us what you think.", "And you?"]

> **Friendship – prompt questions**
>
> How do you know if you can trust someone?
> Do friends ever argue with one another?
> Would you tell your friends your biggest secrets and worries?
> Would you prefer a friend who is funny but unreliable or reliable but serious?

Thank you. That is the end of the test.
[Ensure candidates DO NOT leave the room with the candidate booklet.]

B1 Speaking and Listening

This test should not exceed 22 minutes.

> *Please note:* With the exception of the Task Sheets in Phases 2a and 2b, this sample test frame will be used only by the Examiner. It will not be shown to the candidates.

3 minutes   Phase 1a

Hello. My name is _____ (Examiner).

[Ask Candidate A and Candidate B in turn questions about name and nationality (see below).]

Name	What's your name? Can you spell it for me?
Nationality	Where do you come from? How long have you lived here?

Thank you. Could I have your marksheets? *[Collect marksheets.]*

Thank you.

Now you are going to ask each other some questions. I want you to find out from each other some details about your family. You have two minutes to talk to each other.

[Withdraw eye contact to signal that candidates should start. Allow two minutes. Prompt candidates with questions from the box below, or others suitable for the level, if necessary (e.g. if interaction breaks down or if language remains below B1 level).]

> **Prompt questions:**
>
> Do you come from a big or small family?
>
> Which do you think is more important – family or friends?
>
> How would you describe the personality of your close family members?
>
> Does your family live in the UK? (If not: Where do they live? Do you think they'll visit you one day?)

Thank you.

7 minutes   Phase 1b

In this part of the test, you are each going to talk for about one and a half minutes. While you are talking, your partner will listen to you. Your partner will then ask you three questions about what you have said.

_____ (Candidate A), **you're going to tell** _____ (Candidate B) **about your favourite possession and why it is so important to you.**

_____ (Candidate B), **you're going to tell** _____ (Candidate A) **about someone you thought of as a role model growing up and why you admired them.**

You both have one minute to think about what you want to say. You can make notes if you want to. _[Indicate paper and pencil.]_ **If there's anything you don't understand, please ask me.**

[Withdraw eye contact to signal start of preparation. Allow 1 minute for preparation.]

_____ (Candidate A), **are you ready? Please tell** _____ (Candidate B) **about your favourite possession and why it is so important to you.** _____ (Candidate B), **listen, and ask three questions at the end.** _[Allow 1½ minutes.]_

Thank you. _____ (Candidate B), **please ask** _____ (Candidate A) **your questions now.**

Thank you.

_____ (Candidate B), **are you ready? Please tell** _____ (Candidate A) **about someone you thought of as a role model growing up and why you admired them.** _____ (Candidate A), **listen, and ask three questions at the end.** _[Allow 1½ minutes.]_

Thank you. _____ (Candidate A), **please ask** _____ (Candidate B) **your questions now.**

Thank you.

Test 5

Test 5

5 minutes   **Phase 2a**

In this part of the test, you are going to listen to two recordings and answer some questions. You can make notes [indicate paper] if you want to.

You hear two messages from different places. [Hand each candidate the booklet open at the correct page.] Where is the speaker? In a city, in the mountains or beside the sea?

Where is the speaker?

        in a city   in the mountains   beside the sea

Listen to the information. [Play CD.]

_____ (Candidate A), **in the first recording, where is the speaker? In a city, in the mountains or beside the sea?**

Thank you.

_____ (Candidate B), **in the second recording, where is the speaker? In a city, in the mountains or beside the sea?**

Thank you. [Retrieve booklets.]

Now listen again, and answer these questions.

_____ (Candidate B), **in the first recording, what is the speaker excited about?** [short pause] **And what are they doing tomorrow?**

_____ (Candidate A), **in the second recording, how long was the train journey?** [short pause] **And what did they do today?**

[Play CD again: scripts as above. At the end of the recording ask each candidate in turn their two questions again. After **each** question, **wait** for the candidate's response.]

Thank you.

7 minutes overall   Phase 2b

✻ **3 minutes**

Now you're going to plan something together.

I'd like you to imagine that you work for the local council and you have an investment to make. *[Hand out candidate booklet at correct page.]*

First talk together about which project you should build and choose the one you think would be best for your area. *[Read out list while pointing at the first box.]*

Then plan and decide what to do about these things. *[Read out list while pointing at the second box.]*

You have two minutes to talk about this, so don't worry if I interrupt you.

[Withdraw eye contact to signal that candidates should start. If candidates do not start within 10 seconds, ask: **Would you like to start now?***]*

Which project?	Plan and decide
• a new youth centre • a new health centre • a new shopping centre	• where to build • what facilities to have • the opening hours

Thank you.
[Retrieve candidate booklets.]

✻ **4 minutes**

Now you're going to talk together about lifestyles. Talk to each other about how living in the city is different to living in the countryside, and which you'd prefer.

[Repeat if necessary. Withdraw eye contact to signal start of activity.

If necessary, prompt candidates with questions from the box below (e.g. if students are experiencing difficulty in continuing the interaction or if they stray from the topic). Adapt if necessary. Encourage candidate-candidate interaction by eliciting agreement or alternative opinions from candidates by asking questions such as "What do you think?", "Tell us what you think.", "And you?"]

> **Differences between countryside and city life – prompt questions**
>
> Are the transport services in the city better or worse than those in the countryside?
>
> Would you feel safer living in the city or the countryside?
>
> Where is it probably easier to get a job – the city or the countryside? Why?
>
> If you lived in the countryside, would you have the same number of facilities as in the city?

Thank you. That is the end of the test.
[Ensure candidates DO NOT leave the room with the candidate booklet.]

Test 6

B1 Speaking and Listening

This test should not exceed 22 minutes.

> *Please note:* With the exception of the Task Sheets in Phases 2a and 2b, this sample test frame will be used only by the Examiner. It will not be shown to the candidates.

3 minutes   Phase 1a

Hello. My name is _____ (Examiner).

[Ask Candidate A and Candidate B in turn questions about name and nationality (see below).]

Name	What's your name? Can you spell it for me?
Nationality	Where do you come from? How long have you lived here?

Thank you. Could I have your marksheets? *[Collect marksheets.]*

Thank you.

Now you are going to ask each other some questions. I want you to find out from each other about your diet and what kind of food you like to eat. You have two minutes to talk to each other.

[Withdraw eye contact to signal that candidates should start. Allow two minutes. Prompt candidates with questions from the box below, or others suitable for the level, if necessary (e.g. if interaction breaks down or if language remains below B1 level).]

> Prompt questions:
>
> What are your favourite and least favourite foods?
>
> Which do you think is more important – the taste of food or how healthy it is?
>
> Would you rather eat a home-cooked meal or a meal at a restaurant? Why?
>
> Have you ever thought about becoming a vegetarian?

Thank you.

7 minutes **Phase 1b**

In this part of the test, you are each going to talk for about one and a half minutes. While you are talking, your partner will listen to you. Your partner will then ask you three questions about what you have said.

_____ (Candidate A), **you're going to tell** _____ (Candidate B) **about an event that changed the way you think about life and how it changed it.**

_____ (Candidate B), **you're going to tell** _____ (Candidate A) **about a place you would love to visit and why you want to go there.**

You both have one minute to think about what you want to say. You can make notes if you want to. [Indicate paper and pencil.] **If there's anything you don't understand, please ask me.**

[Withdraw eye contact to signal start of preparation. Allow 1 minute for preparation.]

_____ (Candidate A), **are you ready? Please tell** _____ (Candidate B) **about an event that changed the way you think about life and how it changed it.** _____ (Candidate B), **listen, and ask three questions at the end.** [Allow 1½ minutes.]

Thank you. _____ (Candidate B), **please ask** _____ (Candidate A) **your questions now.**

Thank you.

_____ (Candidate B), **are you ready? Please tell** _____ (Candidate A) **about a place you would love to visit and why you want to go there.** _____ (Candidate A), **listen, and ask three questions at the end.** [Allow 1½ minutes.]

Thank you. _____ (Candidate A), **please ask** _____ (Candidate B) **your questions now.**

Thank you.

5 minutes   **Phase 2a**

In this part of the test, you are going to listen to two recordings and answer some questions. You can make notes [indicate paper] **if you want to.**

You hear two answerphone messages. [Hand each candidate the booklet open at the correct page.]
Where is each speaker? The dentist's, the doctor's or the pharmacy?

Where is each speaker?

      the dentist's   the doctor's   the pharmacy

Listen to the information. [Play CD.]

_____ (Candidate A), **in the first recording, where is each speaker?**
The dentist's, the doctor's or the pharmacy?

Thank you.

_____ (Candidate B), **in the second recording, where is each speaker?**
The dentist's, the doctor's or the pharmacy?

Thank you. [Retrieve booklets.]

Now listen again, and answer these questions.

_____ (Candidate B), **in the first recording, what time does Alice expect to get to work?** [short pause] **And what does she want Jack to do about the customer?**

_____ (Candidate A), **in the second recording, what time does Larry now expect Olivia's appointment to be at?** [short pause] **And what will Olivia do after her appointment?**

[Play CD again: scripts as above. At the end of the recording ask each candidate in turn their two questions again. After **each** question, **wait** for the candidate's response.]

Thank you.

7 minutes overall   Phase 2b

✳ **3 minutes**

Now you're going to plan something together.

I'd like you to imagine that you work for the local council. You have money to spend on one new care project. *[Hand out candidate booklet at correct page.]*

First talk together about the different projects and choose the option you think would be best. *[Read out list while pointing at the first box.]*

Then plan and decide what to do about these things. *[Read out list while pointing at the second box.]*

You have two minutes to talk about this, so don't worry if I interrupt you.

[Withdraw eye contact to signal that candidates should start. If candidates do not start within 10 seconds, ask: **Would you like to start now?***]*

Which care project?	Plan and decide
• a new home for the elderly • a new animal shelter • a shelter for street children	• where in your town/city to build it • what facilities to provide • who to open it (e.g. a famous person)

Thank you.
[Retrieve candidate booklets.]

✳ **4 minutes**

Now you're going to talk together about health. Talk to each other about the healthcare facilities where you live and how they could be improved.

[Repeat if necessary. Withdraw eye contact to signal start of activity.

If necessary, prompt candidates with questions from the box below (e.g. if students are experiencing difficulty in continuing the interaction or if they stray from the topic). Adapt if necessary. Encourage candidate-candidate interaction by eliciting agreement or alternative opinions from candidates by asking questions such as "What do you think?", "Tell us what you think.", "And you?"]

> **Health facilities where you live – prompt questions**
>
> How far from you is the nearest hospital, doctor's practice, dentist's, pharmacy, etc.?
> Is healthcare free where you live? If not, how much does it cost? Is it expensive?
> If you had millions of pounds to invest in healthcare, what would you spend it on?
> What do you think about plastic surgery? Is it important to provide this service?

Thank you. That is the end of the test.
[Ensure candidates DO NOT leave the room with the candidate booklet.]

Test 6

IELTS Life Skills Level B1 - Exam Practice Units - Audioscripts

Unit 1
Listening script 1:

Male: I used to love going to the cinema with my wife Alison at weekends. It was something relaxing yet simple. There's no planning or stress involved, is there? We used to be film fanatics! That all changed, though, when I got a health check. It wasn't good news. I needed to get out and about more and do some exercise or I would have serious health problems, the doctor warned. So I gave up the cinema and the butter popcorn for a healthier, more active lifestyle. I tried hill walking with Alison first but I didn't really enjoy it because of my fear of heights. Then, my boss at work invited me to play golf with him. It was love at first swing! I never thought it possible, but now I actually prefer playing golf to watching films.

Listening script 2:

Male: I used to be a professional footballer some years ago. I was pretty good. I played in League One. Sportiness runs in my family, you see. My dad used to play rugby for England when he was younger. The problem for my dad, though, was that when his rugby career ended, he didn't know what to do with himself. He got depressed and had some serious issues. I learned from his experience, though, so before I retired from football, I already had a plan for another career. I'd used my free time while playing football to qualify as a mountain guide, so I started up a guiding business after I left football. Why mountain guiding? Well, I used to love going up the mountains with my grandfather as a kid. Those were my happiest memories.

Unit 2
Listening script 1:

Next week's going to start off very cloudy and windy. On Monday, the sun's going to go into hiding and it's not going to return until midweek. But at least Monday's going to be mostly dry. There are only going to be a few showers. The showers are going to disappear completely on Tuesday. It's still going to be very cloudy, but it's going to feel milder as the wind's not going to be as strong. Wednesday's going to be a beautiful day without a cloud in the sky. It will feel quite hot, compared to the temperatures of recent weeks. Wednesday's definitely going to be the best day of the week, but Thursday and Friday are going to be fairly good too. There's going to be a little more cloud in the sky and it won't feel quite as warm, but it's still going to be very pleasant.

Listening script 2:

It's going to be very cold on Monday as strong north-easterly winds bring cold air down over the UK. And it's not going to be pleasant at all because heavy rain showers are also expected throughout the day. Tuesday's going to be even worse. Heavy rain's going to fall during the morning and this is later going to turn to sleet and then snow. On Wednesday morning, it's possible that much of the country's going to wake up to a covering of snow on the ground and continued heavy snowfall. However, this is going to turn back to rain by midday as the temperature starts to rise. By Thursday morning, all the snow's going to be gone, but the wet and windy weather's going to remain with us until the end of the week, sadly.

Unit 3
Listening script 1:

Female: It was the most amazing two weeks of my life. From the moment we stepped off the boat, everything was perfect. We'd travelled by boat because of my husband's fear of flying. Isn't it strange how someone can have a fear of being on a plane but love doing crazy things, like canoeing in fast-flowing rivers and climbing huge cliffs? The most incredible experience we had was when we were mountain biking on Denali and we saw a mountain lion about twenty feet away. It was huge. I guess I should have been scared but all I could think to do was take a photo of it! Luckily, it ran back into the forest and left us alone after I got the picture. We had the most perfect end to our holiday too: a horse riding tour around Wonder Lake.

Listening script 2:

I can't think of a better way to holiday. It's so comfortable and you have the most beautiful view out of your window when you wake up each morning; I never get tired of looking out at the sea. At first, I thought I wouldn't like it as I used to get sea sick when I was younger, but technology has advanced now and even in bad weather you don't feel the effects of the big waves. The most amazing memory I have is of my trip to the Antarctic. Seeing penguins and seals on the ice and dolphins and whales in the sea was incredible. The most perfect part was waking up one morning, looking out my cabin window and seeing a group of orcas playing beside the ship. It was magical. What an adventure!

IELTS Life Skills Level B1 - Exam Practice Units - Audioscripts

Unit 4
Listening script 1:

Male: It started when I woke up one morning before work. I took some pills, pain killers, you know? And I thought that would solve the problem, but I wasn't able to clear my mind or think properly all day. I couldn't concentrate, so I had to come home from work. By the evening it felt like my brain was on fire. My wife started to get scared when she noticed my face was getting swollen. That's when she called the ambulance. I was rushed to the Accident and Emergency centre. I'd never been there before and hopefully never will again. What an awful place; people with terrible injuries everywhere. One had a bad break and his arm was in a cast; another was holding her back in a lot of pain. I was seen first because my condition looked serious, but it turned out to be an allergic reaction and I was fine the next day.

Listening script 2:

Skiing is a lot of fun, but it's not exactly risk free. If you fall badly, you can hurt yourself. Usually that means a broken arm or leg, or something more serious like a broken back. But there are other risks, too. I was in Levi, a ski resort in northern Finland and it was freezing cold. I made sure I wore three layers on my top half and two layers of pants. I also had my hat, scarf and a woolly pair of socks. The problem was I'd left my face uncovered. As you ski, the wind hits you really hard. It was minus 10 degrees but it felt like minus 20. By the end of my first run down the slopes, I felt uncomfortable. I made the mistake of not stopping, though and skied on for the rest of the day. Well, when I got back to the hotel that evening, my face was numb and above my eyes there was a terrible ache. I felt a pain in my head for about two days afterwards – and I never made the same mistake again.

Unit 5
Listening script 1:

Female: We'd both had a long day at work and we hadn't got much food in the house so we decided not to stay in and cook. We went to a place by the sea. Our friend, Michelle, had recommended it to us the week before. She said the main courses were very tasty. We were surprised, though, when we looked at the menu. It wasn't what we were expecting at all. It read like a takeaway restaurant; burger and chips, sausage, beans and chips and so on. Not exactly gourmet food, we thought! But we were completely wrong. I've never had such a delicious plate of burger and chips before. It might have sounded like takeaway food, but it definitely didn't taste like it. My husband, Donny, was just as impressed with his fish and chips. He said it was the best he'd ever had.

Listening script 2:

Female: I suggested we get a takeaway. 'Why don't we just pick something up on the way home?' I said. After all, we'd had a really long day. The kids had had a fantastic time at the amusement park, but now we were all tired and hungry. But my husband, Angelo, is a chef and he doesn't think the quality of takeaway is very good at all. At first, he wanted to go home and cook something up but the kids and I were getting really impatient and we didn't want to wait another hour or more for something to eat. Eventually, he agreed that we could stop at a nice-looking place on the way home to get something for home. The food was OK, I guess, but the biggest shock was the bill. My chicken alone cost £20. We left feeling very disappointed. 'OK … Next time, let's just cook at home,' Angelo said. 'That was a waste of money.'

Unit 6
Listening script 1:

I find there are more and more delays these days on the road, you know? Every day I get stuck in traffic jams on my way to work. Then, I look to my left and see all the taxis using the bus lane and it makes me a little annoyed. Why can't I use it too? The reason I still drive despite the traffic, roadworks and all the other delays is because it gives me independence. I can leave work at any time and I don't have to worry about when the next train is coming, you know? I just open the door, get in and drive off. Even if my daily journey gets longer and longer, I definitely won't change how I travel to work. I mean, who wants to spend an hour on a crowded train with no seat room every morning? At least I can turn on the radio, relax and listen to some music and I've always got somewhere to sit!

Listening script 2:

Female: It is very expensive and I probably won't travel to work this way anymore when the company stops paying. It's just one of the conditions of my job contract that I get free travel by any method I want to use for the first three months. I have to say, it's been great. I can sit in the back seat relaxing and planning my day ahead – and it's comfortable, private and actually quite quick as the drivers can use the bus lane. What's not to like? What will I do when my three months are up? Well, I'll probably get the train every day. I think I'd rather drive but I haven't got my licence and I definitely won't have time to take the test before then. I'll definitely take it soon, though. I like the idea of not having to worry about the train schedule. Driving gives you so much more independence.

IELTS Life Skills Level B1 - Exam Practice Units - Audioscripts

Unit 7
Listening script 1:

Female: It must be nearly 25 years that we've been good friends – like best friends, really. Marie feels more like a sister to me than an aunt. There are only three years in age between us. That's because my mum comes from a really big family of ten kids. Mum's 22 years older than Marie. Marie's the youngest and Mum's the eldest of grandma's children. I first started to hang out with Marie when I was 9 and she was 12. We'd just moved to her area and were close neighbours, so we saw each other all the time. It was the start of a lasting friendship. I don't see the rest of family very much, which is quite sad. I mean, I've got lots of cousins I don't even know. But Marie and I have been close ever since.

Listening script 2:

Male: James and I lived in the same home because Aunt May and Uncle Tommy looked after me when I was growing up. You see, my parents died when I was very young. Although I'm an only child, I think of James as my brother after all the time we've spent together. Growing up, I think Aunt May and Uncle Tommy felt bad about me losing my parents because they were never as strict with me as they were with James. I used to do some crazy things and not get in trouble. James wasn't jealous, though. I think he was just happy to have another boy around. Aunt May and Uncle Tommy had five kids of their own, all of whom were girls except James. We're the same age and even today James and I like exactly the same things.

Unit 8
Listening script 1:

Female: My happiest memories are from the earliest years of my education. After that, everything got very serious and stressful; all study and exams. My class at school had about 30 pupils in it. We all came from the same little village, so we were friends both inside and outside of school. That made my very first day of school really easy. Why would I be nervous when I already knew everyone? 18 years ago, schools looked like very different places than today. There were no interactive whiteboards or tablet computers; the teacher wrote with chalk on the blackboard and we wrote with pens or pencils or crayons when we were colouring. Those were the days! If you could colour, draw, paint and play games throughout your education, wouldn't school be so much more fun?

Listening script 2:

Female: If I'm honest, I never really liked school while I was in it. I couldn't wait to get out into the real world and be independent and free! But that soon changed when I finished university and had to find a real job and deal with responsibility. Now I look back and think of all the happy times I had, especially in my teenage years. It seemed boring at the time; all those long study sessions getting ready for the 'big' exams to make sure we did well and got a good place in university. But, actually, all the hard work we did together and how we helped each other out and cheered one another up when we were stressed created the friendships that are still my most special ones today. If I could go back in time, I would love to do it all again.

IELTS Life Skills Level B1 - Practice Tests - Audioscripts

Test 1
Listening script 1:
Attention passengers. Boarding is now complete. Please make your way to the upper decks. I would like to remind you that access to the car deck is not allowed during the crossing. Unfortunately, the captain is unwell. There will therefore be a slight delay to this sailing while we wait for our new captain to arrive. The 8:30pm to Dublin will now leave at 8:55pm. We apologise for this delay. By way of apology, we are offering all passengers one free sandwich and hot drink. You may collect your free sandwich and drink from the bar on Deck 7, the restaurant on Deck 8 or the club lounge on Deck 9.

Listening script 2:
Hello. This is an announcement for Nora Lynch, Nora Lynch. Nora, please come to the Airport Information Desk as soon as possible. Your vehicle, registration X88 HNT, is parked at the exit to the short-term car park. As a result, no other vehicles can get in or out of the parking area. Please report to the information desk by 10:25. The time is now 10:15 – you have ten minutes. If you do not report within the next ten minutes, the police will take your vehicle away and you will have to pay £100 to get it back. Nora Lynch, X88 HNT, please report to the Airport Information Desk now. Thank you.

Test 2
Listening script 1:
Hi. It's Dawn. I'm just ringing to see if you're free for something last minute. Remember that short city break that Jeff and I were looking forward to? Well, he's had to cancel due to some important work meeting. Typical! Anyway, I was thinking, rather than go on my own, would you be around? We fly out Thursday evening, so you'd only need to take Friday off, as you'd be back in time for work on Monday. What do you think? The weather forecast's fantastic – glorious sunshine and not a cloud in the sky! We could see all the famous sights and go for a cruise on the canal. Come on! What do you say? Let's have an adventure!

Listening script 2:
Hi Alice! It's Rod. I've been looking at the weather forecast for next week and it's not great. Monday to Wednesday is going to be a washout – heavy rain every day and high winds. Thursday and Friday have showers forecast too. It only gets dry at the weekend. Oh … I hope the sun comes out for us. How can we do all the exciting outdoors things and adventures that we've planned if the weather's awful? I know rain won't stop some of the activities going ahead, but they sure won't be as much fun. I was thinking, though: should we delay our surfing lessons till the weekend? I don't want to be learning to surf in those high winds forecast for early in the week. Let me know what you think.

Test 3
Listening script 1:
Female: Hi Mike. It's Fi. Sorry, love. I'm going to be late home from work again. There was a fight on one of the floors and I've had to take a young lad who was badly cut to hospital to get stitches. You know, Mike, sometimes I get really depressed doing this job. Looking at that poor young boy today, I felt so sorry for him. He's in jail for shoplifting. Is he really a criminal? I mean, even the fight today wasn't his fault. He accidentally bumped into someone and apologized, but they attacked him anyway. I think I'm going to write a letter to the editor of the local newspaper about this. Surely, we should be helping young people who make small mistakes improve their lives not locking them up with real criminals.

Listening script 2:
Male: Hi Sara. It's just Phil. Good news: I'll be back home soon. I've just sent my final report in to the editor and my flight leaves tomorrow. I can't wait to see you. Writing about the situation here has been so depressing. Yesterday, I saw two nurses carrying a young child into the hospital. He was badly hurt but luckily the doctors were able to save him. I hope whoever did that gets sent to prison for a very long time. Isn't war terrible? I think my career really needs a change of direction after this. I've always wanted to write a sports column. I mean, I'm qualified to comment, aren't I? After all, I played football professionally for a while. I'm going to talk to the newspaper about changing departments when I get back.

Test 4
Listening script 1:
Male: Hi! It's just me. Traffic's awful, so I'm running very late. There was an accident on the motorway and a lorry is stuck in the middle of the road. Anyway, I was supposed to pick your mum up from the hairdresser's at 6 but she texted me to say she'll probably be finished by about 5.30 now. If you could collect her for me, you'd be the best daughter in the world. Rach usually waits for me in the shopping centre and when I meet her we go for a coffee, but she'll wait outside the hairdresser's today so you don't have to pay for parking. OK? Thanks a million.

IELTS Life Skills Level B1 - Practice Tests - Audioscripts

Listening script 2:
Male: Hi! Just ringing to welcome you back. Hope you had a great time in Spain. I bet you're glad you booked two weeks rather than one, right? So much more time to enjoy the place. Dad must've been a happy man when he picked you up from the airport. You know, he's really missed you while you've been away. I think he was lonely. It's the first time you've gone on holiday without him. He even invited me over for Sunday lunch – and would you believe he did the cooking? That's a sure sign something was wrong – Dad hates cooking! You did all of it when I was growing up.

Test 5
Listening script 1:
Female: Hello, Karl! It's Priya here. I arrived about three hours ago – just in time to see the sun set over the valley. The weather's beautiful and the forecast for the rest of the week is great. Mostly sunshine and blue skies, but there's even some snow expected at the end of the week, which I'm very excited about. We've put up our tents on some high, flat ground near a lake. The night-time view there is beautiful. Below us, in the distance, we can see all the lights of the homes in the valley. Above us, the sky is dark and clear and the stars are twinkling. We've changed our plans for tomorrow. We wanted to climb the highest peak immediately, but it looks very difficult, so we've decided to hire a guide to help us improve our climbing skills now instead.

Listening script 2:
Hi Nicki! We finally made it! We got a taxi out of the city centre to the train station. That took about a quarter of an hour. Then it was a four-hour train journey to the campsite. I can't tell you how I excited I was when I finally saw the waves crashing onto the beach in the distance because that meant we were nearly there. We put our tents up on the sand, then lit a fire and had a barbecue. Then we went to bed early as everyone was quite tired after the long journey. This morning, the weather was awful, and we thought about going all the way back to the city to the indoor sports centre just for something to do, but, luckily, the sun came out at 12 and we were able to play some water polo.

Test 6
Listening script 1:
Female: Jack, it's Alice. Just to let you know I won't be at work for the meeting by 10 o'clock like I said. It's definitely going to be at least a half hour later now before I arrive. I've had to stop for a prescription for my daughter, Ellie. She came home from school yesterday evening very sick and we took her to the doctor's. He gave me some medicine to give to her last night and a prescription to get when the shops opened this morning. Anyway, I'm here now waiting to collect it and I'll be in to work as soon as I can. Don't cancel the meeting, just give the customer a 'long' tour of the building and then serve some tea and biscuits. Jack, you're a star!

Listening script 2:
Male: Michelle, it's Larry. The dentist couldn't find anything wrong when we visited her earlier this morning; she said the ache must be coming from Olivia's mouth rather than her teeth. She recommended this doctor, though. He's an ear, nose and throat specialist. I'm in the waiting room now with Olivia. There's a long list of patients, though, and this could take a while. We've got an appointment for 11 o'clock, but the receptionist says the delay is about a half hour. After we've been seen, I'm not taking Olivia into school. She's too unwell, Michelle. I'll bring her over to Gran's house. She can mind her while I go back to work.

IELTS Life Skills Level B1 - Preparation Sections - Answer Key

Section 1
Play - Do - Go
Exercise 1
1. Tennis 2. Archery 3. Hiking
4. Badminton 5. Hockey 6. Yoga
7. Shopping 8.Aerobics 9. Cycling
10. Fishing

Exercise 2
A. Do: martial arts; puzzles; pilates
Play: baseball; football; volleyball; golf
Go: snowboarding; swimming; hill
walking; skiing; surfing
B. Do: aerobics; yoga; archery
Play: tennis; badminton; hockey
Go: hiking; shopping; cycling; fishing

Used to
Exercise 1
A. don't do anymore
B. Question: Did ... use to **Short
answer:** ✓ did ✗ didn't **Positive:**
used to **Negative:** didn't use to

Exercise 2
A. 1. Have a barbecue 2. Go to the
shopping centre 3. Go to music festivals
4. Go camping 5. Go to the cinema
6. Sit around the campfire singing

Section 2
Hot and cold
Exercise 1
A. 1. Boiling 2. Hot 3. Warm 4. Mild
5. Cool 6. Cold 7. Freezing
B. 1. Spring 2. Summer
3. Autumn 4. Winter

Raining cats and dogs
Exercise 1
A. 1. Windy 2. Snowing 3. Raining
4. Sunny 5. Drizzle 6. Foggy 7. Hail
8. Sleety 9. Thunder 10. Cloudy
B. Snowy / Raining; Rain / Hailing /
Sleeting; Sleet / Cloudy / Thunder /
Sunny / Drizzling; Drizzle / Foggy /
Wind
C. 1. It is 2. It is 3. There is
4. It is 5. There is 6. It is

Be going to – weather forecast
Exercise 1
A/B. Question: is ... going to
Answer: (for weather verbs):
✓ 's going to ✗ 's not going to rain
(for weather adjectives):
✓ 's going to be ✗ 's not going to be
(for weather nouns):
✓ 's going to be ✗ 's not going to be
✓ are going to be ✗ are not going to
be
C. Showers
D. 1. It is going to be 2. It is going to
be 3. There is going to be
4. It is going to 5. There is going to be
6. It is going to

Section 3
Dream holidays!
Exercise 1
1. Sun 2. City 3. Adventure
4. Activity 5. Weekend 6. Safari 7.
Shopping 8. Family 9. Camping 10.
Spa 11. Cruise 12. Snow

Countryside versus City
Exercise 1
A. (Suggested answers)
Countryside: scenery; wildlife; sunset;
waterfall; farmland; coast; cave; cot-
tage; wood; stream; river; village; valley
City: library; museum; palace; café;
department store; gallery; theatre; the
underground; skyscraper; pedestrian
zone; river; stadium **Both:** harbour;
river; castle

A. (Suggested answers)
Countryside: going horse riding;
going fishing; going hillwalking;
doing adventure sports; doing snow
sports; going mountain biking; taking a
tour of the castle; **City:** going on an
open-top bus tour; going sightseeing;
visiting famous landmarks; going to an
exhibition; going to a play; going to a
musical; visiting Chinatown; visiting
parliament; going on the big wheel;
going to the amusements;
Both: going sightseeing; doing adventure sports; doing water sports; visiting
a theme park; seeing ancient sites;
visiting famous landmarks; taking a tour
of the castle

C. Noisier / More interesting /
Friendlier (more friendly) / Healthier
(more healthy) / More dangerous /
More popular / Safer / More boring /
Bigger / More polluted / More beautiful /
Cleaner / More modern
D. 2. The city is more polluted than the
countryside. 3. The countryside is
more boring than the city. 4. The city
is more dangerous than the countryside. 5. The countryside is more beautiful than the city. 6. The city is noisier
than the countryside. 7. The city is
more modern than the countryside.
8. The countryside is friendlier than the
city.

The best memories!
Exercise 1
The worst / The funniest / The bravest
/ The most amazing / The most unusual

Exercise 2
A. Question: Have / visited
Short answer: ✓ have ✗ haven't

Positive form: have / visited
Negative form: have / visited
B. 1. have ... done 2. has ... happened

3. have ... had 4. have ... visited
5. have ... had

Section 4
I feel ill
Exercise 1
A. 1. Bleeding 2. Temperature
3. Broken arm 4. Earache
5. Headache 6. Backache 7. Sore
throat 8. Toothache 9. Stomach ache
10. Fever
B. 1. a/e 2. a/e 3. d 4. b 5. c
C. 1. must 2. should 3. mustn't 4.
don't have to 5. have to

What should I do?
Exercise 1
1. Tablet/pill/medicine 2. Plaster
3. Brain 4. Operation 5. Fever
6. Swollen 7. Bone 8. Ambulance
9. Cut 10. Bandage 11. Cough
12. Cold 13. Accident 14. Pharmacy

Exersice 2
A. 1. get 2. see 3. go to 4. go to
5. get 6. make 7. call 8. take
9. have 10. put 11. take 12. put

Section 5
First course
Exersice 1
1. Mushroom soup 2. Spinach and
cheese pie 3. Lettuce and tomato
salad 4. Garlic bread 5. Melon
6. Cheese snacks

Exersice 2
1. will 2. shall 3. wouldn't
4. isn't 5. doesn't 6. aren't
7. wasn't 8. shouldn't

Second course
Exersice 1
1. Salmon and baby potatoes
2. Burger and chips 3. Steak, baby
carrots and potatoes 4. Vegetarian
pizza 5. Barbecued sausages and roast
potatoes 6. Cheesy pasta and broccoli
7. Toasted tuna sandwiches
8. Chicken curry and rice 9. Cheese
omelette 10. Lamb and lemon rice

Exersice 2
1. How about a fish dish as well? /

IELTS Life Skills Level B1 - Preparation Sections - Answer Key

Why don't we have salmon and baby potatoes? / What about a meat dish too? 2. What do you think? / Have you any suggestions? / Does that sound OK?

Third course
Exersice 1
1. Cheesecake 2. Fruit salad
3. Ice cream 4. Chocolate cookies
5. Coconut cream pie
6. Strawberry yoghurt

Exersice 2
1. should 2. Let's 3. doesn't
4. wouldn't

Shopping list
Exercise 1
A. 1. any 2. a few 3. many 4. some 5. some 6. no 7. lots of 8. much 9. some 10. much 11. a 12. some
C. 1. Coffee 2. Tea 3. Soft drinks
4. Wine 5. Beer 6. Lemonade

Section 6
How do I get there
Exercise 1
A. 1. by car 2. on foot 3. by tram
4. by taxi 5. by train 6. by ferry
7. by coach 8. by bus 9. on the underground 10. by bike
B. 1. take 2. the 3. the 4. go
C. ..., rarely, occasionally, sometimes often, usually, ...

By road
Exercise 1
B. 1. b 2. c 3. d 4. a
C. 1. Before 'hitchhike'
2. After 'college' 3. After 'work'
4. Before 'drive' 5. After 'journeys'
6. After 'shops'

Make predictions
Exersice 1
A. Suggested answers: 1. definitely 2. probably 3. probably 4. definitely 5. definitely
B. 1. c 2. a 3. d 4. b 5. e
C. 1. I'll probably 2. I'll definitely
3. Maybe I'll 4. I definitely won't
5. She probably won't

D. **Question:** travel **Short answers:** ✓ I will ✗ I won't **Positive sentence:** travel
Negative sentence: won't travel

Exersice 2
A. 1. a 2. e 3. b 4. c 5. d

Section 7
Who's who
Exersice 1
A. 1. great-grandson 2. great-grandad
3. wife 4. married 5. husband
6. father 7. mother 8. daughter
9. sister 10. brother 11. aunt
12. nephew 13. niece 14. uncle

15. grandmother 16. grandfather
17. son 18. cousin
B. 1. Olivia 2. Nicole 3. Paddy
4. Sheena 5. Julie

Exercise 2
B. 1. o 2. c 3. m 4. l 5. p
6. k 7. q 8. f 9. r 10. j 11. e
12. n 13. i 14. h 15. b 16. d
17. t 18. s 19. g 20. a
C. 1. Confident 2. Serious
3. Negative 4. Rude 5. Calm
D. **Good characteristics:**
reliable; positive/cheerful; polite; friendly; funny; clever; patient; calm; charming; confident; patient; interesting **Bad characteristics:** negative; rude; nervous; cruel
Could be either: serious; fun-loving; crazy; quiet/shy; old-fashioned

My home
Exercise 1
A. **Rooms:** 1. the bedroom 2. the bathroom 3. the kitchen 4. the lounge 5. the sitting room 6. the dining room 7. the hall 8. the cellar
Features: 1. balcony 2. garage
3. bathtub 4. garden 5. private parking 6. conservatory 7. superfast broadband 8. electric shower
9. en-suite bathroom **Appliances:** 1. washing machine 2. microwave 3. dishwasher 4.television 5. oven 6. fridge 7. freezer 8. dryer
9. air conditioning

Section 8
Back to school!
Exersice 1
A. 1. Beginner 2. Elementary
3. Intermediate 4. Advanced
C. 1. Since 2. For

Exersice 2
A. (1) Nursery (2) Primary
(3) Secondary (4) Higher education (University)
B. 1. Facilities 2. Pupils 3. Staff
4. Equipment
C. **Equipment:** whiteboards; tablets; PCs; laptops; projectors; comfortable desks and chairs; good lighting; air conditioning **Facilities:** sports field; changing rooms; canteen; computer lab; Wi-Fi service; clean toilets and showers; study rooms; library; science lab; superfast broadband service; spacious classrooms

Jobs
Exersice 1
A. 1. Butcher 2. Dentist 3. Soldier 4. Director 5. Film star 6. Journalist
7. Judge 8. Mechanic 9. Model
10. Photographer 11. Tennis player
12. Prison officer 13. Security guard

14. Receptionist 15. Nurse

What if...
Exercise 1
A. 1. F 2. F 3. T 4. F
B. **0:** If you are in a similar situation to 12-year-old me, don't give up.
1st: If I ever see her again, I will say a big thank you. / If (or when!) I qualify as a doctor, I will go back to Uganda and volunteer there. **2nd:** If I were you, I would keep trying.
3rd: If I hadn't been part of that programme, life would have been very difficult.
C. work ; get ; move ; will ; return ; were ; study ; could use ; could travel ; would ; would still want ; could ; had ; would have been ; have had ; would ; had been ; might not have tried

Have you got the right qualifications?
Exercise 1
B. 1. what qualifications you
2. you speak any foreign
3. you have worked
4. any other relevant experience you
5. personal qualities are

IELTS Life Skills Level B1 - Exam Practice Units - Answer Key

Unit 1
Phase 2a
Part 1
Listening 1: their leisure activities
Listening 2: their work life

Part 2
Listening 1: a. He needed more active hobbies. b. He was afraid of heights.
Listening 2: a. Because of his dad's bad experience when he finished playing rugby. b. He had happy memories of going up the mountains with his granddad.

Unit 2
Phase 2a
Part 1
Listening 1: mainly dry
Listening 2: mainly wet

Part 2
Listening 1: a. mostly dry – cloudy and windy b. Thursday and Friday are going to be more cloudy and less warm.
Listening 2: a. It's going to be cold with heavy rain showers and strong winds. b. It's going to snow in the morning; the snow's going to turn to rain later in the day.

Unit 3
Part 1
Listening 1: an adventure holiday
Listening 2: a cruise holiday

Part 2
Listening 1: a. Her husband was afraid of flying. b. She took a picture of it and then it ran away.
Listening 2: a. Technology has advanced. b. Seeing a group of orcas playing in the sea outside her cabin window.

Asking questions:
1. How often 2. How many 3. What
4. Who 5. When 6. Why

Unit 4
Part 1
Listening 1: allergy
Listening 2: headache
Part 2
Listening 1: a. His face was getting swollen. b. One day. / He was fine the next day.
Listening 2: a. two layers of pants b. minus ten degrees

Asking questions
1. did … do 2. Did … take 3. Were 4. Have … had 5. Have … been 6. do … feel

Unit 5
Part 1
Listening 1: a restaurant meal
Listening 2: a take-away meal

Part 2
Listening 1: a. Their friend Michelle had recommended it the week before. b. burger and chips
Listening 2: a. at the amusement park b. the expensive food

Unit 6
Part 1
Listening 1: a car
Listening 2: a taxi

Part 2
Listening 1: a. Taxis can use the bus lane and he can't. b. It's crowded and there are no seats.
Listening 2: a. It's a condition of her job contract. b. The train because she doesn't have a driving licence.

Unit 7
Part 1
Listening 1: an aunt
Listening 2: a cousin

Part 2
Listening 1: a. Marie b. 12
Listening 2: a. They weren't as strict with him. b. The speaker was another boy. James had 4 sisters.

Unit 8
Part 1
Listening 1: primary school
Listening 2: secondary school

Part 2
Listening 1: a. She knew all the other students already. b. interactive whiteboards and tablet computers
Listening 2: a. When she finished university and started work. b. They seemed boring.

Answer Key

IELTS Life Skills Level B1 - Practice Tests - Answer Key

Test 1
Part 1
Listening 1: ferry
Listening 2: car

Part 2
Listening 1:
a. 20:55
b. sandwich and hot drink
Listening 2:
a. 10:25
b. police will take vehicle away (and charge £100 for return)

Test 2
Part 1
Listening 1: weekend city break
Listening 2: adventure holiday

Part 2
Listening 1:
a. an important work meeting
b. Thursday evening
Listening 2:
a. heavy rain and high winds
b. because the forecast is good / because there'll be no high winds

Test 3
Part 1
Listening 1: a prison officer
Listening 2: a journalist

Part 2
Listening 1:
a. she had to take someone to hospital
b. write a letter to the editor of her local newspaper
Listening 2:
a. his final report
b. about changing jobs and writing a sports column

Test 4
Part 1
Listening 1: father
Listening 2: son

Part 2
Listening 1:
a. accident on the motorway (lorry in the middle of the road)
b. outside the hairdresser's
Listening 2:
a. 2 weeks
b. his dad cooked Sunday lunch for him but hates cooking

Test 5
Part 1
Listening 1: in the mountains
Listening 2: beside the sea

Part 2
Listening 1:
a. it might snow later in the week
b. hiring a guide to help them improve their climbing skills
Listening 2:
a. 4 hours
b. play water polo

Test 6
Part 1
Listening 1: pharmacy
Listening 2: doctor's

Part 2
Listening 1:
a. around 10.30
b. give them a tour of the building, and tea and biscuits
Listening 2:
a. around 11.30
b. go to her Gran's house

Lightning Source UK Ltd.
Milton Keynes UK
UKOW07f0403170816

280783UK00006BA/17/P